SMART SELLING

SMART SELLING

52 Brilliant Tips and Techniques to Boost Your Sales

Jeff Slutsky

Marc Slutsky

Smart Selling
Cover design by Jeff Slutsky

First published as part of a series of articles in a syndicated column for The Knight- Ridder News Service in 2001-2006.

To order this title online, log on to: www.createspace.com/4411673
ISBN-13: 978-1492226932
ISBN-10: 1492226939

Dedication

To my wife, Helene. She's the best sales person I've ever met and the perfect woman for me.

Contents

Other Books by Jeff Slutsky

- *Smart Marketing* (coauthored with Marc Slutsky)
- *Street Fighter Marketing* (with Marc Slutsky)
- *How to Get Clients* (with Marc Slutsky)
- *Street Fighter Marketing Solutions*
- *The Toastmaster's Guide to Successful Public Speaking* (coauthored with Michael Aun)
- *From the Big Screen to the Real World* (coauthored with Larry Winget)
- *No B.S. Grassroots Marketing* (coauthored with Dan Kennedy)
- *Street Smart Tele-Selling*
- *Streetfighting: Low cost advertising for your business* (coauthored with Woody Woodruff)
- Street Smart Marketing

www.streetfightermarketing.com
800slutsky@gmail.com

Introduction

Smart Selling is based on our Knight-Ridder News Service weekly column, BizSmart. Over the years, these fun and entertaining sales related articles have provided many readers with clever, shrewd and smart tips, hints and anecdotes that help get more sales with less effort. This book is comprised of a collection of many of our favorite articles on sales. With these articles, you'll discover the time-honored inside tricks and techniques from some of the most successful and creative people from around the world. It's presented in a vignette-like format that is sure to keep you interested, motivated, and mesmerized.

Smart Selling provides short chapters. The topics are in all areas of selling and sales and are applicable to many types of business. Your success will come from the adaptation of these ideas to your needs and unique opportunities.

A "Smart Selling Action Plan" is provided at the end of most of the chapters to help you convert the ideas into action. Use these chapters as "thought starters." We want you to get thinking more creatively about your business. But it is your job to take the ideas to the next level. Modify. Adapt. Improve. Make them work for you.

We have conducted many consulting and training programs throughout the country for a variety of businesses, large and small, including McDonald's, Goodyear, Marriott, Chevron, Molson, Subway, Pizza Hut, Sony, Firestone, USPS, and the US Army.

Jeff Slutsky
& Marc Slutsky

For information about keynote speaking, seminars, books and consulting projects, contact Jeff Slutsky at 800slutsky@gmail.com. 800-758-8759 (800-SLUTSKY) web: streetfightermarketing.com.

Chapter 1

Think of Selling Like You Would Dating

Nearly everybody in your organization sells, not just your sales people. You may have to sell a product or service or even an idea. Yet, basic selling techniques are sometimes difficult to grasp. To help understand the basics of selling, think of the selling process as if you were dating. According to Pamela Lanier, President of It's Just Lunch, a Columbus dating service, "Most people share too much information about themselves on a first date." The same thing happens on many first time sales calls.

Prospecting

Like dating, sales first depends on making the initial call. Fear of rejection often keeps us from getting on the phone and asking for that first visit. But, if you don't make the call, you'll never get the date.

Pre-Date

Present your best side. Dress appropriately and if in doubt, error on the upscale side. Be on your best behavior. Mind your manners. You are being judged the entire time. If the first encounter is a lunch, choose a place that's quiet enough to have a conversation and one that has good service.

Qualifying

The first date, like the first sales call, is for qualifying your prospect. This is when most people make their mistake, both in dating and selling. You need to determine if this person meets the key criteria needed to establish a potential relationship. After all, in both situations, you're not looking for a one-night stand.

Probing

Once you qualify your prospect, dig deeper to find out your prospect's needs and wants. Do this before you start sharing too much information about you (or your company and product). If you sense that this prospect is going to be high maintenance, probe some more to see if the ultimate value justifies the extra attention. Don't interrupt when they're talking. You need to interpret what they say with what they really mean.

Objections

As in any sale, there are bound to be objections. You must determine just how critical each objection is. You also need to determine if the objection is legitimate or if your prospect is looking for an excuse to get rid of you. If there is no way to overcome the objection, you may be forced to re-evaluate the potential of the relationship.

Closing The Sale

After an appropriate number of sales calls (or dates) it's time to get their commitment. If all the other steps were handled properly, this should be the easiest part of the process. Sales, like dating, should be a win-win.

Service After The Sale

After the client commits, then it's up to you to make the relationship work. This is often where the hard work comes into play. Just because you have a contract doesn't mean you have to stop working. Don't take it for granted . . . or you may find that your life long customer gets buyers remorse and starts seeking proposals from your competition.

SMART SELLING ACTION PLAN:

- Think of selling like dating.
- Court your prospect.
- Listen intently and ask probing questions.
- Discover likes, dislikes, needs and wants.
- Once you close the sale, continue with good service.

Chapter 2

Using Client Testimonial Letters To Get An Edge

One of the most powerful sales tools you can use is a client testimonial letter telling the world how wonderful you are. And guess what? They cost you nothing to get! There are many uses for these letters especially as an insert in promotional material that is mailed before a sales call, or as part of a leave-behind piece after a sales call.

The best time to get a letter is right after you've completed a good job for a client. Simply say, "You know, I'm very happy that we were able to work with you. It would really be helpful to me if you could send me a brief letter, on your letterhead, with a few of words about how wonderful we were to work with." Most clients are more than happy to accommodate you.

Now, while most clients will agree to write you a letter, in reality, only a few get around to doing it. It's not a high priority for them. If you don't get a letter in a reasonable time you might try calling back. Tell them that you realize they're very busy, and based on your previous conversation, you offer to write the letter for them. They can make changes if necessary. Then they can have it printed out on their letterhead. Or better yet, suggest they send you several pieces of their stationary and you'll have it printed for them, mailed for approval and signature. They can simply get it back to you in the self-addressed, stamped envelope enclosed. Some of the best testimonial letters I got . . . I wrote!

Getting testimonial letters needs to become an ongoing part of your marketing and sales effort. The more you collect, the more ammunition you have. It's also a good idea to cross-index your letters by type of client and perhaps, even by objection. For example, if you're talking to a new potential client and their concern is whether or not, you can meet their deadline, you can provide several letters from previous clients that mention what a great job you did in meeting their difficult deadlines. That enhances your credibility.

To make more impact with your testimonial letters, consider reprinting them to resemble the originals with letterhead quality paper and their logo in color. Better yet, if you have a really strong relationship with your client, ask them to send you a ream of their letterhead. It costs them very little since they probably buy it in huge quantities and will save you a lot of money.

Chapter 3

Doing Business On The Golf Course

Business is often conducted around the game of golf. Whether you're wooing new clients or working your way up the corporate ladder, your behavior and attitude on the golf course can either help or hinder your success. Here are some tips from successful business people who golf for fun and business.

Sig Munster (handicap:10) a Senior Vice President of Morgan Stanley in Columbus, Ohio plays golf with business prospects to size up a person's character, and to see if he wants to do business with that person. There are many behaviors that would be cause for alarm including: cheating on the score; rudeness to the caddy; not raking the sand traps, throwing clubs, miss marking the ball, etc. Munster guesses that 25-30 percent of his business can be attributed to his time on the golf course. "It's a great way to build long term relationships, some which have lasted over 40 years. It gives you something in common with someone." It doesn't matter how good a player you are, according to Munster. It's literally how you play the game that counts when it comes to business. He also feels that membership in a prestigious golf club is also important because it makes it easier for you to attract players, especially top level decision makers.

Steve Miller, (handicap:1.6) President of The Adventure, a Seattle based trade show consulting firm, generally doesn't bring up business on the course unless the client does. He suggests that if you want to bring up business, don't do it too early in the round and don't try to do too much business. Golf is a social event. So being too intense about business can ruin the overall enjoyment of the round. Miller suggests that you should keep current with the PGA Golf Tour, so you can carry on a conversation other than business.

Mark Mayfield, (handicap: 4) a Tucson, AZ based professional speaker, advises letting your guest set the pace with respects to wagering, alcohol and style of play. You'll know after the first green if that person is a stickler with the rules or prefers mulligans and give-me putts. Keep it light. Don't do heavy duty selling on the course, but rather use the time to gather some information and only share a few general points at the most. Mayfield feels that if you give so much information that the client has to take notes and bring their smart phone, you'll probably turn them off. Mayfield shared a story of a very competitive golfer who bet a prospective client $50 a hole. He won the bet but lost the deal.

John McCoy, former Chairman of Bank One. (handicap: no comment).

Smart Selling Action Plan:

- Be on your best behavior. Your character is being evaluated on the golf course. Cheating, temper tantrums, rudeness and other unsportsmanlike conduct will cost you business.

- Join prestigious golf clubs. The higher level of prestige you can afford, the easier it is to attract players, especially higher level decision makers.

- Don't talk business unless your client brings it up. Use the game as a way to build the relationship. Limit the business talk to before or after the round.

- Let the client set the pace. Follow the client's lead with regards to alcohol, betting and style of play.

- Keep current with events on the PGA Tour. It gives you something to talk about.

Chapter 4

The Six Steps to Creating Interactive Voice Mail

(part 1 of 2)

Once you leave a voice mail message, there's no taking it back. When you hear the "beep" it's too late to start thinking about what you're going to say. That's the message from Nashville based Renee Grant-Williams, a nationally recognized voice coach. Renee has trained many top singers on how to use their voice in music including Huey Lewis, The Dixie Chicks, Faith Hill, Linda Ronstadt and many others. Now she's helping business people and executives train their speaking voice to make greater impact.

To create a positive interactive voice mail message know the reason for making the call. Determine how you can get the most out of the call. Here's an example of how the caller accomplishes a very *interactive* message:

Hello, Mr. Mitchell, This is Jeff Slutsky with Street Fighter Marketing. My number is 800-758-8759. It was a pleasure meeting you yesterday, and I just wanted to say that if you choose Street Fighter Marketing to develop your sales and marketing manual for your franchisees, I'll do everything in my power to make the process as painless as possible. I

8

know you have a very busy schedule, but if you could spare a few minutes to return my call, I have some ideas I think you'll find very interesting. My number again is 800-758-8759. Thank you, Mr. Mitchell.

Renee has a six-step checklist that helps you organize your information and create a powerful interactive message:

1. **Know your objectives**. Write down one line that clearly states what you want most to accomplish, change or put into action.

2. **Gather up documents or information.** You might need a product serial number or model number or some other specs. Have that information ready for your message. You may need notes from your last meeting or phone conversation, prices, your schedule, or the new specifications.

3. **Prioritize your goals into a well-planned sequence of topics**. Be sure to write down pertinent facts and figures. Since you never know how long you have on a voice mail message, put your most important information first. Your name, company and phone number are right at the top of that list. Don't assume your listener knows who you are or has your number. Also Renee suggests that it's stronger to say "*This is* Renee Grant-Williams" rather than, "*My name is* Renee Grant-Williams."

4. **Ask the person you're calling for a specific action.** Verbally "highlight" the specific action or actions. State what you want clearly. Include a time frame if appropriate.

5. **Follow up with another call.** Even if the VIP you're trying to reach doesn't return your call, most people usually don't mind if you call again. Let your VIPs know that you understand how busy their lives are by expressing concern for your "call-ee". Always give an out for not returning your call so they don't feel guilty.

6. **Try to get closure.** For example, your message is used to finalize meeting arrangement, " . . .and I will see you then at 4:30 tomorrow afternoon, Thursday the fourth."

Smart Selling Action Plan:

Renee's Six Steps to Interactive Voice Mail Messages:

1. Know and prioritize your objectives.

2. Gather up documents or information.

3. Prioritize your goals into a well-planned sequence of topics.

4. Ask the person you're calling for a *specific* action.

5. Follow up with another call.

6. Try to get closure.

For part 2 of 2, see Chapter 10

Chapter 5

Tips For Taking the "Pro" Out Of Procrastinate

Decision-making is painful. Watch someone trying to make up his or her mind and you'll see just how painful it is to make a decision. For example, watch someone reading a menu. Look at the pained look on his or her face. When you're selling or negotiating, prospects often give reasons to postpone making a decision. However, once you learn to translate the secret language of the procrastinator into simple sales talk, your course of action is simple and effective.

"I need a few more references"

When a client requests additional references or other decision making information *after* you've gotten the order, you have a major problem. That's an indication that your client is not sold or is having second thoughts. Instead of providing information, start asking questions of *why* they need the information. Make sure your tone illustrates your concern and interest in pleasing the client.

"I want to talk it over with my [partner]"

This red flag generally means that you're prospect is not willing to make a decision or has already decided against you and is reluctant to tell you this up front. Follow it up with, "other than wanting to talk it over with your partner, is there any other reason why we couldn't get the go-ahead now?" If there isn't, continue with, "Then let me suggest this: why don't we get the paperwork out of the way now so we can get the ball rolling. Then, you talk it over with your partner (or spouse, or boss, etc) and if there's a problem, just give me a call. Fair enough?" This often helps them move ahead because they usually don't have to talk it over.

"Let me think it over"

They don't have to think it over. They're just not convinced yet. Follow up with, "Tell me, what is the part you need to think over. Is it the price ...the delivery time ...the specs? Once they tell you, go back and start to work your sale again. Ask for more information about the issue for which they said they needed extra time.

"The payment has already been authorized"

We often refer to this as "The Check's In The Mail Syndrome." Though you have the decision the prospect is procrastinating with your payment. This could also happen with your written contract or purchase order. If there is a big lag time between your verbal commitment and the written or financial proof of the commitment, you might have a big problem. When talking to your client, get agreement on a specific deadline to send you the payment or contract. In this way, if it does not arrive by the agreed upon deadline, you know to follow up. Our clients tell us that you should expect to have this kind of problem more often when dealing with smaller companies or individuals.

Smart Selling Action Plan:

- Listen to your prospects carefully for procrastination language.
- Convert what they *say* to what they *mean*.
- Decide on an effective course of action.
- Implement your response to their procrastination empathetic ally.

- Evaluate the effectiveness of your approach and make improvements where necessary.

Chapter 6

Styles of Negotiations

To negotiate effectively, you must try to match the level of resistance you face. Orval Ray Wilson, coauthor of *Guerrilla Negotiating*, suggests that to do this you need to recognize the negotiation style being used by your opponent and adjust your approach accordingly. Orval describes 11 different styles to look for:

Whatever

This person offers no resistance. The guerrilla response is to ask for more than you want. Use this approach when dealing with customers who are dissatisfied and upset, and it really *was* your fault. Just ask, "What would you like me to do?" and wait for their response. Often the adjustment they ask for will be less than the one you would have offered.

Whatever's Fair

Be careful. It's all how you define "fair." Since you'll want to be seen as a fair person you may be overly generous, compromise too much, or concede more than you have to. The guerilla approach is to define "fairness" so that it is to your advantage.

Nice Guy

This person tries to gain advantage under the guise of friendship. To deal with this, maintain your perspective and keep your focus on the *outcome*.

Whiner

This approach appeals to your sympathy. When dealing with a whiner, ask yourself if it's really your problem. If not, don't try to fix it and if it's not relevant to the negotiation, ignore it.

Stonewall

This is when your counterparts become withdrawn and refuses to talk, which is intended to apply pressure. You may become uncomfortable and back off from your position. Your response is to let them be quiet, but fill the dead air time with something else. You can use this approach when they demand detailed explanations of every point of your position. "I'm not discussing it!" is a fair negotiating position.

The Nibbler

Just when you're ready to sign the deal, the *nibbler* will ask for just one more thing. Your response is either to say "no," or if you agree to their request, say that you can give them that *if* they agree to do something for you.

Give-and Take

This is when you can't get a concession, not even a minor one, without demanding a concession as well. To deal with this, keep your reciprocal concessions small and be prepared to make a bunch of them.

Rule Book

The negotiators will focus on the format, placing great importance on the place and time, shape of the table, or the formatting of the documents. The preoccupation with the process is a ploy to distract you from the actual outcome, and you make the mistake of granting real concessions in exchange for mere exception of protocol. Mentally separate the form from the substance. Ask questions concerning their reasons, and request explanations of their position.

Hard Ball

Stubborn, uncompromising, and belligerent. They are unwilling or unable to consider an alternative position. Look for ways to satisfy their core issues without giving in yourself.

Infantile

They want it all. They'll scream like a two-year old. One approach may be to reprimand them. Better yet, find someone else to negotiate with.

SMART SELLING ACTION PLAN:

- When negotiating try to first identify their style of negotiations, based on the examples in this article.
- Once you identify their style, next formulate an appropriate response to their style.
- Should they employ a different style during the negotiation process, modify your response accordingly.
- Never lose sight of the outcome you want to receive from your negotiations.

Chapter 7

Seinfeld Characters For Selling To Different Personalities

Whether selling a product or service to a customer or an idea to a colleague or employee, your results may be improved by first identifying which of the four basic personality types best characterizes that person. According to Cindy Kubica, an interpersonal skills speaker and trainer in Nashville, "The four personality types have been around since Hippocrates. It's been used and over-used by countless sales trainers and management consultants." However, Cindy feels that she has simplified this complicated sales tool by designating each of the four types after a character from the TV sitcom, *Seinfeld*.

The Kramer

Kramers are optimists, extroverts, thinkers, dreamers and doers. They influence people with their enthusiasm. They have a tendency to be "big picture" oriented and are more likely to shoot from the hip. When working with Kramers, don't give too many details. Help them "feel" and "envision" the final result. Other Kramers include Ralph Kramden (*Honeymooners*), Fred Sanford (*Sanford & Son*) and Wile E. Coyote (*Roadrunner*).

The Elaine

Elaines are dominating and directors. Like Kramers, Elaines are also doers, extroverts and optimists. But, they're more self-oriented and want to know as much about the process as the end result. They ruminate over decisions and often second-guess themselves. When selling to an Elaine, give lots of details of "how" they will achieve their end result, step-by-step. Other Elaines include Larry Tate (*Bewitched*), Mr. Drysdale (*The Beverly Hillbillies*) and Mr. Spacely (*The Jetsons*).

The Jerry

Jerrys are generally introverts, low key and good supporters. They have a tendency to be cautious and like consistency. Jerrys become more like Kramers when they're in a totally safe environment. (i.e. Jerry doing stand up.) When selling to a Jerry, stress low risk, avoid pressure tactics, listen a lot, yada, yada, yada. Other Jerrys include Drew Carey, Sheriff, Andy Taylor and Scooby Doo.

The Newman

Newmans are analyzers, conscientious, pessimists, introverts, and doers. When selling to a Newman, give them all the data. Show them charts and graphs. Use logic and limit emotions. Other Newmans include Felix Ungar (*Odd Couple*), Spock or Data *(Star Trek)* and Mr. Peabody (*Bullwinkle*).

What about The George? Cindy said that some personalities cross over between the four types. You get a George by extracting the worst traits of the other four. When possible, avoid Georges, get everything in writing and get paid up front. Other Georges include Frank Burns (*M*A*S*H*), Ted Baxter (*Mary Tyler Moore*), and the Trix Rabbit.

Joe Malarkey a keynoter who bills himself as the *worst* motivational speaker in the world, presents his own satirical version, which he calls "Personality Types: The Three Hour Tour." Joe's unique interpretation uses characters from *Gilligan's Island*. Joe told us, "If you think my idea is ridiculous, then you guys are probably "Professors!"

SMART SELLING ACTION PLAN:

- Make a list of 10 clients (or employees) you work with on a regular basis.

- Place each one of them in one of the four personality profiles. If they cross over between categories, place them in the one that is the closest.

- Try to recall how you've interacted with each of them in the past.

- Knowing the type of personality traits they exhibit, write down some ideas of how you think you could improve your working relationship by relating to them on their level.

- If you don't like using Seinfeld characters, come up with your own fun examples to help you use the techniques.

Chapter 8

Strategies Help You Turn A Presentation Into An Order

You can increase your chances for success when selling your idea, product, service or recommendation using seven strategies for evaluation meetings, according to Alan Weiss, Ph.D. of East Greenwich, RI and author of *Million Dollar Consulting* and *How to Write a Proposal That's Accepted Every Time*. To stand out in a crowd of competitors when selling to a committee, Alan suggests the following:

Learn something about the prospect or buyer that you can use when you are presenting your case. Ask for and review carefully detailed information about the prospect before your appearance. Find "un-obvious" facts that you can utilize to your advantage. Get their annual reports and look on-line for background information with a free service like *www.your paper's website.com* or a subscriber service like *www.hoovers.com*.

Never mention the competition except in positive terms. It's best not to mention the competition at all, whether you know who they are or even suspect. If someone brings them up, be non-committal: "I know of them and have heard they do good work." No one wants to hire a sniper, because you never know when the gun will be turned.

Keep the presentation brief and focus on questions. The group is hearing a lot of people bleat on about how good they are. Make a few quick hits and some relevant war stories and examples, but move quickly to the questions that the group has for you. Your time will be limited, and it's best to deal with what's on their minds, not your mind. This is especially true for recommendations and proposals.

Don't address costs

This is the single greatest error made in evaluation sessions. Someone asks, reasonably, "How much will this cost?" and the individual stammers out some price. Instead, explain that it's *unfair to the evaluators* to cite an investment prematurely. But, you'd be happy to place a proposal in front of them within 24 hours, once you've had a chance to think about what you've learned at this meeting. Invariably, any discussion of costs at this point will kill you.

Use a clever "turnaround" technique

Set yourself apart. Tell the group that, "I tried to put myself in your shoes and come up with the key facts you need to know, so I created this single-page summary as a discussion document for you." Or say, "You're thinking of asking my help to take you from square-one on this project. Let me suggest that you may want to think about square-zero." Do something that will create a phrase associated strictly with you and no one else.

Focus on value

Don't beat to death the value that the client will likely receive from your specific assistance, techniques, methodology, etc. Don't focus on client's merits, focus on the client *outcomes*. Make the client feel good about doing business with you.

Demonstrate professionalism

This should go without saying, but it's often violated. Dress successfully. Shoes shined. Well groomed. At meals, use silverware correctly. Shake hands firmly. According to Ellen Kaye of Perfect Presentations

(Email: Ellen@EllenKaye.com) in a Silicon Valley, California based company that coaches executives to dress and act successfully, "One innocent *faux pas* at an important evaluation meeting can potentially cost your company millions of dollars or hamper your career." Alan also adds, "If you look and act good while you're at the meeting, you're 95 percent of the way to your goals.

SMART SELLING ACTION PLAN:

- Learn about the prospect or buyer.
- Never mention the competition except in positive terms.
- Keep the presentation brief and focus on questions.
- Avoid dealing with costs.
- Use a clever "turnaround" technique.
- Focus on value.
- Demonstrate professionalism.

Chapter 9

Speed The Decision Making Process

Most problems that sales people face with slow decision making are self-created according to David Yoho of Professional Educators, Inc. in Louisville, Kentucky. David feels that we sabotage ourselves when we fail to ask our prospects and ourselves certain questions. If there was no indecision or procrastination, your services would be purchased from a catalog. Ask yourself two questions to improve your results:

1.Do I control the direction, timing and conditions of my conversations?

When prospects control the sales conversation, you're unlikely to obtain a meaningful decision. However, controlling the direction, timing, and conditions of conversations doesn't mean controlling, intimidating or pressuring people. It means asking questions that:
- define solvable problems.
- elicit critical facts.
- create urgency.
- establish credibility.
- obtain feelings, opinions and commitments.
- determine the content and personalization of your value-added proposal.

2. Do I confuse need and want?

People are more likely to decide quickly when they *need* something. However, people need little more than food, clothing, and shelter. Most everything else is a *want*. It is possible to create wants and urgency. Just identify problems and potential solutions that haven't yet occurred to the prospect.

By generating new wants and added value, you can create a unique position for yourself, perhaps as the only acceptable alternative. If you don't create wants and urgency, your prospects will probably decide, "not to decide." And the likelihood that prospects will actually retain your services decreases dramatically the longer they procrastinate.

Four Key Initiatives

Here are four key initiatives that will enable you to speed the decision making process, boost your closing rate, validate your fee and reduce your stress level.

1. Know more about your clients, their situations, and their alternatives than they know about you.

To control the sales conversation you have to know a lot about your prospect before you propose a course of action. Many of us make the mistake of not having a documented set of questions to ask clients. This is somewhat humorous because we all have a documented set of questions once we land the assignment.

2. Learn the prospects' decision making criteria.

If you don't know how prospects are going to make a decision, you're less likely to get one. Simply ask, "What criteria are you going to use to make the decision" or "what do we have to do to land this assignment"? And always obtain a decision date before sending a proposal.

3. Deliver your recommendations and fees directly to decision-makers.

There are decision-makers and decision influencers. You need to know who's making and influencing the if, when, who and what decisions.

A good way to ask is, "Barbara, should you decide to retain my services, you and who else will make the final decision?"

4. Ask a sequence of definitive commitment questions that simplify

the decision making process.

Faster buying decisions are initiated at the moment of first contact. Ask the right questions from the beginning or you're asking for delay. Sometimes, you invest lots of time and money pursuing engagements when you're out of contention.

Prepare and ask for definitive commitments after each major point in your proposition. For example, after explaining your methods of investigation and research, ask if they believe you'll have sufficient information to customize the program.

SMART SELLING ACTION PLAN:

- Next time you're in a selling situation, ask if you or your prospect is in control of the situation.

- Before making a sales call, try to identify the difference between the prospect's *needs* and *wants*.

- Determine who is the real decision-maker early in the sales process.

- Determine the process the prospect goes through when making a decision.

Chapter 10

Smart Messages Can Move Business Forward

(part 2 of 2)

Getting your voice mail message returned is a big challenge since nearly every business uses it. According to Renee Grant-Williams, author of the newly released *Voice Power, Using Your Voice to Captivate, Persuade, and Command Attention,* a quick, effective message is a great time saver. She says your goal in leaving the message should bring you one step closer to the person and the conclusion of business together. Leaving the "right" message depends on both content and delivery. Williams suggests the following steps to leave a professional message that increases your chance of getting your call returned.

Be prepared. Instead of just seeing voice mail as a chance to leave your name and number, see it as a way to advance your cause. You can leave brief details about your product, suggest an idea, or stress the benefits of your service. Be sure to have any documents or information you may need at hand when making the call. Or better yet, make some notes or prepare an outline to insure you leave a strong message without rambling.

Clearly state your information.

Your name, company and telephone number should be stated first. Say your telephone number, clearly, allowing the other person enough time to write it down. Use your full name to identify yourself and it is stronger to say, "This is so-and-so," rather than "My name is."

Ask for a specific action

Rather than just asking someone to call you back, make a specific request. This allows the person to leave you the information you need, if you miss the return call.

Follow-up your initial call

You can call back without being labeled a pest. Let the person know that you understand how busy they are. Saying, "If you're not able to get back to me, I'll try to catch you next week," gives the other person an out. Also, if you are leaving several messages, keep notes on what you said during previous calls. You want your messages to sounds fresh and spontaneous.

Know when to stop talking

Don't ramble just because you haven't been cut off. Remember that you are taking up someone's time. Your message will be appreciated if it is brief and to the point.

Adjust your attitude

Even though you are talking to a machine, you need to speak to the person. The tone of your voice should reflect the content of your message. If you want to convey an upbeat attitude, smile. It will be heard in your voice.

SMART SELLING ACTION PLAN:

You can leave effective messages on voice mail by:
- Clearly state your name, company and telephone number.
- When leaving your phone number, speak slowly.

- Ask your contact to complete a specific action rather than just call you back.
- Follow up with another phone call and leave a time when you will try them back again.
- Keep your messages short and to-the-point.
- Sound confident and don't stumble or allow unnecessary pauses.

Chapter 11

Selling Your Idea To The Boss

There are four questions that all decision makers need answered before they can comfortably and confidently approve any idea, according to Ocala, Florida based speaker and author, Phillip Van Hooser. Providing the answers to these four questions, during your presentation, will help you increase the level of interest in your ideas and get a fair hearing.

Question 1: How much is this going to cost?

It is very difficult for a manager to approve a proposal unless armed with this answer. Therefore, take the time to do your homework up front. Be prepared, but be honest. Never over-estimate or pad the numbers. Others may, but if you wish to earn the right to be heard, the risk is too high. If decision-makers believe you're playing games with them, they may let you play somewhere else.

Question 2: What are the benefits?

This may be the most important question to be answered. *Benefits* serve the decision-maker as both reason and motivation for taking action. Whenever you sell any idea, you should be prepared with as many tangible benefits as possible. However, be careful. Only benefits, which are legitimate and defensible, should be included. Even one benefit that is not legitimate or defensible make the entire list suspect in the mind of the decision-maker. We've found that if you can determine those benefits that are of the greatest concern to your decision maker, you'll also stand a better chance of getting approval.

Question 3: How long will it take?

Time is money. Therefore, you need to offer your decision-makers a realistic expectation of the time required to get your recommendation up and running. However, contrary to Phillip's earlier advice regarding question number one, always overestimate the length of time expected for the project to be completed. Create a specific implementation plan that will allow you to position yourself in such a away as to be under time and under budget.

Question 4: What happens if we don't do it?

After listening to your well-prepared case for a certain action to be taken, you may find that your boss is compelled to consider the downside of the equation. Prepare yourself with a ready response to a predictable question. Phillip suggests a response like, "Boss, If you decide not to approve this proposal, I will accept your decision. However, let me remind you of the benefits, which will not be realized as a result of your decision here today." Then immediately refer to the earlier list of legitimate benefits.

Even using these four questions as background for your proposal, your boss may not give you approval. However, even if you don't get approval every time, you may still be successful getting quality "face time" with the appropriate decision maker. And that's your first step to a "yes."

SMART SELLING ACTION PLAN:

Phillip Van Hooser's four questions or getting your proposal taken seriously:
* Question 1: How much is going to cost?

- Question 2: What are the benefits?
- Question 3: How long will it take?
- Question 4: What happens if we don't do it?

Chapter 12

Sell The End Result, Not the Process With A *Benefit Statement*

When you're introducing your product or service to a potential customer you want to capture their attention immediately. The best way to do that is to tell this prospect the "end result" of having used your product or service. In our case, we would <u>not</u> say, "we conduct seminars, workshops, and consulting projects in local marketing and telephone selling." That tells our prospect just enough information so he or she can tell us they're not interested. Instead, you stress the unique benefits of your products and services to your prospect.

One of the most challenging benefit statements we developed was for a life insurance agency. The minute someone says they sell life insurance, people head for the doors. It seems that nobody wants to talk to a life insurance salesperson.

The challenge was to create a benefit statement that would grab a prospect's attention and avoid the turn-off associated with life insurance pitch. You can test your benefit statement at a party. In a conversation, when someone asks you what you do, the benefit statement should cause them to response with, "no kidding ... how do you do that?" In essence they're asking you to give a sales pitch about your product or service.

In the case of the life insurance sales person, one of his major areas of concentration is helping well to do people have a significant retirement income. So, the benefit statement developed was, "We specialize in helping people accumulate over a million dollars for retirement with only a small monthly contribution." Nowhere did you hear the word "life insurance."

Ask yourself, what do you do that clients will find very valuable? How can you phrase it so that, when asked, most people will response with, "No kidding. How do you do that?"

For example, if you merely said that you're an accountant or a CPA that might be of some interest. On the other hand if you said, "I specialize in helping people dramatically reduce their tax bill." that would get most people's attention. The fact that you're a CPA will come up later in the conversation. If you stress CPA than you're automatically lumped in with all the other CPAs.

A stockbroker might say, "I specialize in uncovering undervalued companies with strong long term potential for people who want to maximize their investment profits."

The branch manager of a local bank might say, "I specialize in helping businesses handle just about all their finance needs including establishing lines of credit and cash flow management." He sells loans, CDs and checking accounts but that's irrelevant. What's important is the result, the benefit of this banker's services.

SMART SELLING ACTION PLAN:

- Write down all of the benefits or the end results a prospect may expect after using your product or service.

- Create your own benefit statement using the following format: "I specialize in (benefit) without (negative)."

- Practice using your benefit statement when you meet people. Work it into conversations and gage their reaction to it.

- Modify your benefit statement as needed for specific products and services or for different types of prospects.

Chapter 13

Sell Your Unsold Inventory In Your Sleep On Ebay

You can make money in your sleep by selling your unsold inventory on Ebay, according to Helene Eichenwald, a successful Kansas City based "e-tailer." Eichenwald points out several advantages of this approach for any kind of business with merchandise on the books:

- Generates additional cash flow at very little expense and effort
- Avoids conditioning your regular retail customers from waiting for close-outs and major mark-downs.
- Expands your market globally.
- Allows you to market using your off-peak times.

To be successful on Ebay, Eichenwald has the following tips:

Use multiple photographs of the product.

You get one free photo and each additional one is 15 cents. When selling higher ticket items, consider paying the extra. Show it from several angles, especially all tags and original packaging. Since buyers can't see the product first hand, you need to prove that it's new and in mint condition. Using a digital camera or existing JPEG files, you can easily upload the photos for your auction. Eichenwald will often use up to six different photos of the same item to draw more attention. She also suggests you use a title bar picture which lets bidders view your item immediately by displaying a picture in the top left corner of your listing.

Use a strong title

You only have 45 characters in the title, which is what most people search by. Use the most critical words. There are several well-known abbreviations: "NIB" (New In Box) and "NWT" (New With Tags). If the item is a brand name, put that in the title as well as key words that describe it. Include the regular suggested retail price.

Use a detailed description

Think of your item from your buyers' perspective. You want to use strong selling copy just like an ad or a catalog description. Suggest ways the item can be used. When giving a feature, follow it with a benefit.

Make it easy for your customers to buy

Elect to use one of the Ebay payment programs, which makes it easier and safer for both buyers and sellers. For a small percentage *Paypal* allows the buyer to use a credit card and the net payment will then be deposited directly into your business checking account. When payment is confirmed you'll receive an e-mail and you can ship the item.

List your item(s) in multiple categories for greater exposure

For example, we listed our *Street Fighter Neighborhood Sales Builders* audio album under "books – audio" and "books - self help." Using Eichenwald's approach, our first album sold in seven days.

Sell brand name, popular items

The more the buyers are familiar with your products, the easier it is to sell. Remember, they will be comparing your offering to the same item at retail. To get an idea of how to set your minimum bid, go on Ebay and search for similar items to see how they're priced and displayed.

Smart Selling Action Plan:

- Go on Ebay and look around to get familiar with it.
- Search for items that might be similar to items you can offer.
- Take one brand name item and list it on Ebay.
- Create a strong title, body copy and several photos for the item.
- Start making a list of items you would like to remove from inventory for future auctions.

Chapter 14

Sell It With Seminars

The advantages of using seminars as a marketing and sales tool, according to Michael Aun, coauthor of *The Toastmasters International Guide to Successful Speaking* are:

- It puts you in front of potential clients.
- Gives you credibility.
- Positions you as an expert.
- It's free.

When Dr. Gary Berebitsky was just starting his pediatrics practice after finishing his residency in Phoenix, he used free seminars to help his practice through its infancy. His hospital sponsored prenatal care seminars for expectant mothers and he taught those seminars, free. It was a great public service for the hospital and Dr. Berebitsky who both acquired new patients because of the combined effort.

Frank Foster, patent attorney, was asked to speak at the Ohio Speaker's Forum. This is a group of professional speakers who also write and produce original material. One of their biggest concerns is protecting intellectual property. Mr. Foster's seminar, at this group's meeting, was an excellent way to attract potential clients who may need legal work done in this area.

Target Audience

Mr. Aun suggests that you first need to identify your ideal target audience. What type of customers or clients do you want to attract?

People Magnet

Once you've determined the type of target audience you want, identify what they have in common and look for groups that have meetings where these potential prospects attend.

Outline

Next, you need to figure out what you want to say. It's important to give your audience valuable information they can use but not give away the store at the same time. You also must *not* be a constant commercial. Depending on the amount of time you have, you need to figure out what you want to accomplish in this presentation. What are the main points you wish to make?

Practice

Find a no-liability group to whom you can practice. This practice group ideally should have no one in the audience that you would normally go after as a client. Use this group to work out the bugs in your presentation, and the butterflies out of your stomach. Don't expect to give a polished presentation immediately. That's okay. That's part of the process. Another good way to improve your presentation skills is to join a local Toastmaster's club.

Handouts

With every presentation, prepare a leave-behind piece that your prospects can take home with them. It can be a combination of bullet points, fill-in-the-blanks, and illustrations if appropriate. Also, make sure that your name, business, address, and phone appear at the top or bottom of every sheet in your handout. Make it easy for people to get in touch with you later. If you have a Power Point to go along with your program, you can provide a printout of your slides as a reminder of your content.

SMART SELLING ACTION PLAN:

- Outline a 1-2 hour seminar that educates people about your product or service.
- Develop a audience handout, based on the seminar outline.
- Practice your seminar with several groups of people that typically don't buy from you.
- Join your local Toastmasters club to help learn presentation skills.
- Identify the target group you want to present this seminar.
- Identify organizations that have meetings that reach that target group.
- Contact that group and offer to provide a free seminar.

Chapter 15

Sales Contests Reward Both the Business and its Employees

Would a reward of a trip for two to Las Vegas get you to work a little harder? That's exactly what Rick Winnestaffer did with his company, WinnScapes, a landscape and design firm based in the Columbus-area. He held a sales contest for five of his employees as a way to generate more sales during the month of May. By the end of the month he saw a 15 to 20 percent jump in sales.

A sales contest can be a great way to kick off a new product or capitalize on your company's best selling opportunities. A contest cannot only boost your sales but it can also show your employees how much you value their time and effort. Winnestaffer offered the following suggestions for running a sales contest.

Pick a time frame with high sales

Ultimately, you want your employees to have success. Instead of picking weeks or months where sales are generally lower, pick a time that captures your best selling opportunity. Then, challenge your sellers to set new records for sales during that time frame. Just like you want to advertise when you're busy, capitalize on your best selling opportunity.

Have well-stated goals

You can't run a fair contest by just going out and saying, "Sell as much as you can." Look at where your employees have been previously and set individual goals that commensurate with their experience and the type of product they sell. Make sure the goals are reasonable and attainable in order to have your employees feel like they are having success.

Have a worthwhile incentive

Winnestaffer came up with some great rewards for his employees. The first place seller received a trip for two to Las Vegas, Nevada; second place received a trip for two to Niagara Falls and third place received dinner for two. Not only did Winnestaffer say he'd do it again but that next time he'd run a two-month contest with even bigger prizes.

Track the contest accurately and timely

Define the rules up front and stick with them. Keep track of where employees are in relation to their sales goals and post the current results in a visible location so everyone knows where they stand.

Supply the rewards quickly

The rewards should be given quickly; no more than a few weeks after the contest is over. It is even better if you can reward someone during the peak-season when breaks are both needed and deserved. WinnScapes allowed their employees to take their vacations in the summer, a peak time for landscaping.

Competition can work well within an organization

In this case, it made the day-to-day selling process more exciting. It broke up the routine of a normal month at work and the friendly competition even helped to bring employees together. Offering meaningful rewards also helps with retention and gives employees an edge up on their peers. Finally, it helps everyone realize that they might be able to reach a higher potential.

SMART SELLING ACTION PLAN:

To have a successful sales contest:
- Pick a time when sales are generally high.
- Set individual goals for employees.
- Create meaningful rewards.
- Define the rules and stick with them.
- Reward employees quickly, even at peak times.

Chapter 16

Recruiting Quality Tele-Marketers

Telemarketing and telephone selling can be a powerful addition to your Street Fighter arsenal. But one of the most challenging areas of building up an effective telephone selling force is finding people who can actually sell over the phone. Well, here's an idea that was taught to me by good friend, George Walther, author of *Phone Power* and *Upside Down Marketing*. He suggested that I run a small ad in the local newspaper or a brief posting with the on-line recruiting website. that simply said, "Position available. Great pay. Call this number for details." The candidates will call that number and get an answering machine with an outbound message that went something like this:

"If you're looking for a sales position with unlimited potential, you've dialed the right number. This is Jeff Slutsky, President of Street Fighter Marketing, and in the next five minutes I'll give you a detailed description of the positions we have available. Toward the end of this message I'll then outline for you our compensation package including the hourly wages, bonus program, commission structure and other special perks we offer. I'll be sharing a lot of information with you so feel free to call this number back as often as you like and you might even want to take some notes. Then, if you like what you hear, call back one more time and leave us a detailed audio resume right here on our machine. Now keep in mind that we are offering a telephone sales position so "sell" us on why we should call you back for an interview . . . ."

At that point, I start giving details about the position. The neat thing about this approach is that you're not flooded with a bunch useless resumes because it's practically impossible tell if someone can sell by a piece of paper. Only those who are reasonably serious will even bother to leave you a message. Of those, only a fraction will be worth following up with based on their response. Remember, you're only concerned with their selling skills over phone. You don't care how they look or dress or who they know. If they communicate clearly with a strong selling message on why they're worth interviewing, you have a good candidate.

Go ahead and set up the first interview, but do it over the phone, too. Then, if that goes well, you bring them in for an in person interview. Of course, it's a good idea to run any recruiting practice by a labor attorney to make sure you're in compliance with all state and federal laws.

You can also try a similar approach with Skype. Have them log on to a YouTube video of your job description. Then have them record their response and email it to you. Sometimes you learn a lot by looking into their eyes.

Chapter 17

Prospecting for Customer Gold

Looking for new prospects? Who isn't? Just about every business spends a big chunk of its marketing budget looking for people who might want to buy its products or services.

Amazingly, many businesses overlook a group of prospects that already want to buy their products and services — their current customers! Kelly Borth, president of Greencrest, a full service marketing, advertising and public relations agency, says prospecting your existing customer base is like panning for nuggets downstream from a gold mine. You know the gold is there; it's just a question of finding it.

If you're like many business owners, you've fallen into a comfortable groove with your customers. You sell them the same thing again and again without taking the time to explore their needs the way you would with a new customer. Or you let time go by after the sale without keeping in touch. The result? Your sales are flat, and your customers don't appreciate the full value of doing business with you.

Borth offered these tips for maximizing the prospectability of your existing client base:

Survey your customers.

Find out as much as you can about their perception of your

relationship. Ask what they like about your products or services and what they appreciate about doing business with you. Ask if you're meeting their expectations. If they say you're not, ask what you could do to *exceed* their expectations. Ask how they perceive your company in relation to competitors. This kind of benchmark survey can best be performed by an independent marketing agency so that the customers feel free to answer candidly. Customers who are thrilled with your company can be solicited to provide testimonials. Give extra attention to customers who express dissatisfaction.

Communicate all of your products or services

As your company evolves, you add new products and services that existing customers might not know about. Make sure your customers know everything you can do for them. Otherwise, you might find that they're buying from a competitor, simply because they don't know you can fill that need.

Collaborate with customers

Looking for new product or service ideas? Work with your existing customers. Product development tailored to your customer base is a lot easier than launching new products into an uncharted market. Asking key customers for input into the future of your business model or product line is a great way to build trust.

Keep in touch

Remind your customer of all the benefits of doing business with you. A well-crafted newsletter is a great way to educate clients about your company and what you can do for them. You can do this faster and cheaper electronically with a service like Constant Contact. A direct mail or e-mail campaign with a timely offer can increase repeat orders. Posting valuable content on your Web site gives customers a reason to visit on a regular basis. Introduce clients to networking contacts who can increase their business. Corporate open houses, golf outings *(see Chapter 3)* and client-only events offer other opportunities to cement relationships.

SMART SELLING ACTION PLAN:

- Survey your customers.
- Communicate your full product line.
- Collaborate.
- Keep in touch

Chapter 18

Maximize Existing Accounts Easier Than Getting New Ones

Your selling success depends on your ability to penetrate the larger accounts you already have, according to Paul S. Goldner, author of *Red-Hot Customers: How to Get Them. How to Keep Them.* This does not mean you shouldn't prospect, however, once you make your first small sale to an account, you will likely be better off fully penetrating it. Paul offers six principles of account maximization:

Know Your Customer's Business

Every customer business has five distinct business segments:
1. The receipt of inbound shipments of raw materials
2. The manufacturing process
3. The shipping of goods to customers
4. The marketing and sale of finished goods to customers
5. The service of finished goods for customers

It's also important to understand the market within which they operate. Instead of trying to sell your products and services, you must position yourself to make your customers more successful.

Become Part of Your Customer's Organization

It's great to see the face behind the voice. Take every opportunity to integrate your company into the operations of the customer's account.

Become a Consultant to Your Customer

The benefit you sell is the "potential product or service," which is the actual product or service delivered by your company and all of the value you can layer onto it. There are six sources of value:
1. Business know-how
2. Supply chain optimization
3. Operational support
4. Ease of doing business
5. Organizational strength
6. Product or service design

Create a Good Operational Process

This falls in the suggestion of "ease of doing business" mentioned above and can be a tremendous source of value for your customer. When you develop a new customer relationship, take the time to make certain that the transaction-processing elements are in order in the following areas:
- Know who to send your invoices to.
- Let the customer know where to send the checks
- Make sure all the required information your customer needs is on the invoice including your phone number.
- Make it easy for the customer to place orders.
- Make it easy for the customer to receive technical service.
- Return calls in one business day.
- Find out what else you can do to make the relationship more effective

Work Your Account at All Levels

There are four buying influences within an organization:

1. The facilitator
2. The certifier
3. The user
4. The check signer

Look at the customer's organization from a cross-functional perspective. Get to know the department vice presidents and departmental secretaries in addition to the traditional contacts. This can help you develop support for your product and service. Paul reminds us that a 'yes' can come from only one influence within the organization. However a 'no' can come from anywhere.

Leverage Your Relationships

Take your successes in one department within a company and use them to create successes in other areas within the company. Don't forget to consider your customer's parent company, subsidiaries, joint ventures and even other vendors.

SMART SELLING ACTION PLAN:

- Know Your Customer's Business.
- Become Part of Your Customer's Organization.
- Become a Consultant to Your Customer.
- Create a Good Operational Process.
- Work Your Account at All Levels.
- Leverage Your Relationships.

Chapter 19

Increase Average Purchase To Improve The Bottom Line

Suggest-selling is a simple and inexpensive marketing technique used at the time of a purchase to increase sales and profitability. It is often relatively easy to add 10 to 20 percent more to an existing sale or get an existing customer to buy just one more item.

Consider the restaurant that despite having really great banana cream pie had very weak dessert sales. To motivate his wait staff to suggest dessert more aggressively, he ran a contest. For one month, the server who sold the most banana cream pies would win…one banana cream pie. And they would get to throw it in the owner's face! You never saw such a motivated crew in your life. Just by getting them to suggest dessert, the restaurant's dessert sales increased nearly 50 perecent during the contest and a residual increase of 20 percent thereafter.

An ice cream manufacturer in Canada wanted to promote its product more aggressively through a convenience store chain. They offered to provide to the chain a contest enticing their employees to suggest-sell the ice cream bars at the cash register during a purchase. It was suggested that the ice cream company use a mystery shopper approach where each store would be visited several times during the month. If the employee suggested an ice cream bar to the mystery shopper, that employee was handed a $50 bill on the spot. If they failed, they were handed a printed note telling them they just lost $50 but they may get another chance. A contest like this creates excitement for employees and as soon as someone wins some cash, the word spreads.

Suggest-selling doesn't have to be limited to food items or contests. A good example from a service business is the approach we use in our own business. Once a client has booked one of us for a sales or marketing seminar for a meeting or convention, our sales people offer to sell copies of our popular books, *Street Fighter Marketing,* and *Street Fighter Marketing Solutions* in quantity for the attendees. When books are purchased as an "add-on" to a speaking contract, the client gets them for less then half of the retail price. This happens about one-third of the time and generally adds about another 50 percent to that sale. Those clients get a great price for the books, their attendees walk away with something tangible in their hands from the seminar and we increase our sales.

Smart Selling Action Plan

- For impulse items, use a fun contest to entice employees to make the suggestions.
- For bigger ticket add on sales, aggressively price the add on product or service too.
- Motivate the buyer to agree to the additional purchase.
- Suggest those products or services that have a wide appeal to your customer base.
- Choose items that aren't normally bought. You don't want to cannibalize your sales, rather, you wish to increase your average sale.
- Structure the upsell process so it is easy to buy. If it takes too much explanation, you might not get the level of cooperation from employees that you would like.
- Support the upsell effort with signage, displays, buttons and other collateral material that might get the customer to ask, while reminding the employee to suggest.

Chapter 20

In Selling, All The World's A Stage

You can dramatically increase your communications effectiveness by applying some techniques used by professional actors, according to Ellen Kaye a New York trained professional actress. Her company, Silicon Valley, California based Perfect Presentations, is a presentation, communication and image consulting organization which transforms many Fortune 500 executives into more effective presenters and leaders.

Ellen, drawing upon her experiences as one of the top actors in New York, teaches that actors are trained to convince *you* of *their* reality. Likewise, you can use the same mental exercises she did to convince millions she had a pounding headache when she really didn't; or she was having the "time of her life" with Kathie Lee and Frank on a Carnival Cruise® (when she really had a pounding headache.) Likewise, you can use those same brain drills just prior to visiting a customer, colleague or boss, to help you get past those emotional blocks that zap your effectiveness. When you walk through the door for an important meeting, it's like the camera rolling during a major shoot.

Emotional Memory

When you're selling you have to be at your best, whether you feel like it or not. Just before a scene, actors often briefly visualize a pleasant experience from their past. Ellen suggests that just before an important meeting, close your eyes and recall how good you felt during a special experience. Then open your eyes and charge forward with the same feeling fresh in your mind.

Substitution

This acting technique is used when actors have a challenge working with another actor. For example, it's very difficult to show the proper emotion during a love scene when the person you're pretending to be head over heels causes you to relive your lunch. To get into character, the actor might mentally substitute the undesirable partner with one he or she does like. In selling or managing, you may have to have a good working relationship with people that are difficult. So next time you find yourself in this situation, mentally substitute the person you like for the one you dislike.

Immediate Previous Circumstance

Actors know that their entire outlook and emotional state leading up to the next scene is determined by events that just happened. If you're headed into an important meeting or making a critical sales presentation, and you just found out your company announced a major restructuring, you may have difficulty being persuasive. Ellen suggests that you create a positive immediate previous circumstance before your presentation or meeting. For example, most sales people like to celebrate after a big sale. That's a waste of a powerful immediate previous circumstance. The time to go after a big sale is right after you've made one. Your immediate previous circumstance is so positive that you stand a much better chance of getting another sale.

Smart Selling Action Plan

- Write down three very positive experiences that you've had this past year.
- Practice "emotional memory" with each one to see which

memory works best for you.

- Write down two of your favorite clients or colleagues.

- Practice "substitution" with two difficult clients or colleagues

- To create a positive "Immediate previous circumstance" before an important meeting recall a specific event in which you had the feeling you need now.

- For more info about her services, contact Ellen: Phone: 650-963-9874; Email: Ellen@EllenKaye.com

Chapter 21

How To Get Customers To Buy More By Buying You

How customers feel about people that serve or sell them is a key factor in winning and keeping them, according to Dr. Michael LeBoeuf. In Dr. LeBoeuf's best selling book, *How To Win Customers and Keep Them for Life*, he suggests that every time you boost your customer's self image you make a significant stride in keeping that customer for life. Here are five of Dr. LeBoeuf's specific ideas to help you do that:

1. Develop a genuine interest and admiration for your customers. The more you know and admire about your customers, the easier it is to win them over. Get them to talk about themselves and listen with your undivided attention. A good rule of thumb is to let them do 80 percent of the talking. Your customers are much more likely to buy when they're doing the talking and when you're doing the listening.

2. Recognize and praise people for what they want to be recognized and praised for. With a little observation and common sense it's easy to spot what people want to be complimented for. If you notice that a customer has lost weight, has a suntan, or a has a new hair style, acknowledge and compliment it. Two main points need to be stressed about the art of giving compliments. The first is that they must be sincere. Your customers know when they're being conned. Second,

make them specific. If possible, find a way to compliment your customer for something that results in having used your products and services in the past.

3. Put them at ease and establish rapport. Your customers prefer the company of people who make them feel accepted and relaxed. There are a number of specific kinds of behavior that contribute to establishing personal rapport:

Smile sincerely. Not a false, paste-on smile, but one that starts with your eyes.

Keep a relaxed, open stance

Lean slightly toward your customer, being careful not to invade his or her personal space.

Maintain eye contact. Your customers will consider you more confident, honest, and knowledgeable.

If appropriate, occasionally touch the person in a non-threatening manner.

Know the customer's name and use it when you speak to him or her.

Subtly mirror the customer's behavior

Match his or her rate of breathing and speaking. Assume a similar posture.

4. Use humor where it's relevant and appropriate. Laughter is a tremendous influence tool. The most effective humor is brief and self-effacing. The shorter the story, the greater the impact.

5. Let them know that you're thinking about them. Send your customers congratulatory cards for birthdays, promotions, graduations, or anything you can congratulate them for. Keep a list of their professional and personal interests, and if you see an article that would be of interest, clip it out and send it with a brief, handwritten note.

Smart Selling Action Plan:

• Develop a genuine interest and admiration for your customers.

• Recognize and praise people for what they want to be

recognized and praised for.

- Put them at ease and establish rapport.
- Use humor where it's relevant and appropriate.
- Let them know that you're thinking about them.

Chapter 22

How Titans Sell By Becoming A Value Resource

How many ways are there to sell? There are countless variations, of course, but Ron Karr, author of *The Titan Principle*, believes that when you come right down to it, there are really only five basic selling styles:

- **Commodity**

- **Display**

- **Stimulus/Response**

- **Consultative**

- **Relationship**

In Commodity Selling there is only one basis for the consumer's decision: price. If you don't have the lowest price, you lose. In Display and Stimulus/Response styles of selling the decision to buy is based on impulse. "Impulse" means the customer makes a fast decision based on immediate circumstance, with very little input needed from the seller. For most sales people, impulse buys don't happen as much as they would like. *Titans*, according to Ron, spend most of their selling time in the top two styles: Consultive selling and Relationship-based selling. These two styles sell solutions. In Consultative selling, you concentrate on uncovering your customers' challenges so you can prescribe the right cure. In Relationship-based selling, you rely on the strength of your relationship and personality to get the sale. Ron suggests that they both have advantages and you should use both.

Positioning

You have very little time during the sales call to capture the attention of your prospective customers. Titan selling begins the moment you first make contact with that prospect which is when you position yourself. A *position* is how the customer compares you against your competition. Most sales people use three methods to position themselves with prospects:

1. Position by Title
2. Position by Product or Service
3. Position by Resource.

In most cases, positioning yourself by title or products and services leads to price selling where there is little room to set yourself apart or differentiate from your competitors. True differentiation occurs only when you position yourself as a *resource* to your customers. Distinguish yourself from your competition by highlighting the results your customers get from using your unique mix of products and services.

As a resource you must address at least one of the following areas:

- Increase your customer's profits
- Increase your customer's productivity
- Reduce your customer's operating expenses
- Help your customer maintain a competitive edge

There are six main areas where you can add value to your prospect or customer's operation:

1. Information.

Knowledge you or someone in your organization has about events and trends in the prospect or customer's industry.

2. Distribution.

Your organization's ability to get a product from point A to point B.

3. Systems.

Your organization's ability to electronically support your customers and streamline their buying process.

4. Stabilities.

Your organization's area of strength that provide additional comfort and value to your customers.

5. Product or Service Design.

Your organization's ability to set up and implement superior solutions.

6. Assets for Key Customers.

Critical financial, technical, or interpersonal tools your organization can provide your customers in special situations.

SMART SELLING ACTION PLAN

- Develop a selling style that is a comfortable mix of "consultative" and "relationship"
- List ten specific resources you have available to you now that your customers would find valuable
- Over the next month, start offering yourself as a resource to help your customers improve their profits, productivity, operating expenses, and/or maintain a competitive edge
- List five customers who would benefit from information you have about their industry.

Chapter 23

Hollywood Inspired Negotiation Tactics

Movies provide some of the greatest examples of effective negotiation tactics. For example, in *Glengarry Glen Ross*, there's a scene where Al Pacino loses a sale because Kevin Spacey volunteers information in front of Pacino's client without knowing the details of the negotiations. Pacino later tells Spacey, "*You never open your mouth until you know what the shot is.*" We always teach our clients that you never volunteer unsolicited information because it's often used in objections later on.

Al Pacino's brother, James Caan (Sonny) in *The Godfather,* was censured by his father, Marlon Brando (Vito Corleone) after they finished their meeting with Al Lettieri (Sollozzo). He tells his son, "*don't ever let the other person know what you're thinking.*" During that meeting, Sonny voiced interest in Sollozzo's idea to invest in narcotics, even though Vito was against it. Sonny's obvious interest lead to the attempted assassination of his father. Now, hopefully, making such a negotiation faux pas won't lead to such drastic measures in your mediations, but it could mean the death of your deal. It's better you should just "*make them an offer they can't refuse.*"

Volunteering unsolicited information also got Mary McDonnell in trouble in, *Sneakers*. Mary goes undercover to date an employee at the corporate headquarters where Robert Redford's team breaks into. She's caught by Ben Kingsley, the computer genius bad guy and boss of the geek she's "dating." Ben buys her story at first and she's let go. As she is leaving, she casually mentions that she'll never go out on another computer date. Kingsley immediately determines that no computer would have matched those two, and her cover is blown. She should have followed the advice of Jack Nicholson to Karen Black in *Five Easy Pieces* when he says, "*If you wouldn't open your mouth, everything would be just fine.*"

John Patrick Dolan, author of *Negotiate Like The Pros*, references *Weekend at Bernie's* in his seminars. Although Bernie is dead, nobody seems to notice. While propped up on a sofa at a party, dead Bernie receives an offer to buy his Porsche for $35,000. Bernie's silent. Minutes later he's offered $40,000. Bernie says nothing. Then he's offered $45,000. Silence. Even with the offer, tops $55,000, Bernie still says nothing. According to John, if we all acted more like Bernie we'd put a lot more life in our negotiations.

When you move toward the end of the negotiations or the "close" you might follow the tactics presented by Paul Newman in *The Verdict*. He says, "*Never ask a question unless you have the answer to it.*" When you get to the "closing" phase of negotiations, you're trying to get agreement. The only difference is that in a negotiation, the client is the judge and jury. One way to work toward a final "yes" is by asking a series of questions that will always get you a "yes." This movie quote points out a very important underlying element in successful negotiations, which is to simply do your homework before talking.

Goal setting

In this scene, Rocky convinced himself that he couldn't win the fight so he sets a new goal. By "going the distance," he can feel that he was a success because he achieved his goal. But, it's possible that he might just have sold himself short. On the other hand, if Rocky's goal was to beat Apollo Creed, he might have. However, he never even gave himself a chance. Conversely, Apollo Creed set his goal when he said "*I'll drop him in six.*" This was after ignoring concerns from his trainer who noticed Rocky's unusual training method of punching raw sides of beef. It seems that the message is, that if you set a goal, you should first gather all the pertinent information about the project. Apollo did not reach his goal even though he won the fight. Rocky lost the fight but made his goal. Rocky must have been watching Clint Eastwood (Dirty Harry Callahan) in *Magnum Force*, when he said, "*A man's got to know his limitations.*"

Unfortunately many people set their goals based on the fear of unrealized expectations. If Rocky set his goal to beat Apollo and only went the distance, he might have felt like a loser. But, because he was unwilling to take that emotional risk of setting his sights higher, he has to wait until *Rocky II* to finally beat Apollo. The relationship between expectations and goal setting was never more obvious than in the movie *Horse Feathers*, when Groucho said to Zeppo, "*I married your mother because I wanted children. Imagine my disappointment when you arrived.*"

SMART SELLING ACTION PLAN

- Rent a number of your favorite movies.
- As you're watching, look for scenes with effective negotiation tactics.
- Write your favorite quotes on individual index cards and review them next time you start a negotiation.
- Also look for quotes in other areas like customer service, leadership, time management, teamwork, etc.

Chapter 24

High Impact Selling Techniques

To be successful selling, you need a plan, says William T. Brooks Greensboro, N.C. based author of *High Impact Selling: Power Strategies For Successful Selling.* Bill was a college football coach who said that the only way his teams could win, consistently, was to:

Establish a simple, well-conceived "game plan" that took maximum advantage of the unique skills of his players.

Drill it so firmly into his players' heads that they could follow it without having to think about what they where doing; and

Insist that it be followed in every detail. Bill feels that you can be successful selling using the same formula.

Bill's selling system contains only six steps that take you from prospecting to closing and each step is expressed in a common word or phrase using the acronym I.M.P.A.C.T:

Investigate

To get a large range of qualified prospects for what you are selling. The better job of finding qualified prospects you do, the higher your closing average will be.

To get all the information you need about those prospects so you can be very convincing. Ask enough of the right questions, of the right persons, in the right places, and you'll always have plenty of qualified prospects.

To prepare your strongest and most persuasive presentation.

Meet

To set up the best selling situation.

To make your prospects feel important and relaxed.

To start them talking about themselves.

To gain rapport.

Probe

To discover what your potential clients want most. The best way to serve your own interest is to put the needs and desires of your customers first.

To uncover real and perceived needs. To deliver value to your prospects, you must first see yourself primarily as a value resource for your prospects.

To get them involved in the selling process.

To assess their buying style.

Apply

To show prospective buyers that you understand their needs and desires. Do this by choosing the most appropriate product or service.

To present the product or service that will fulfill those needs and desires. Do this by tailoring your sales presentation to your prospects' needs and wants. Make intangible values tangible using a little creativity.

To let them experience how the product or service meets their needs and desires.

To make sure they understand what benefits they will receive from ownership.

Convince

To validate and prove every claim you have made. Never make

a claim you can't back up with facts. If you can prove it, show your evidence.

To answer any questions prospective buyers may have.

To justify the price by emphasizing value.

To reemphasize the importance of customers' desires and relieve any fears of buying.

Tie it down

To negotiate a win-win agreement.

To welcome, identify, and answer all objections.

To reinforce customers' positive feelings about buying.

To close the sale by asking for the order. Ask them to buy now.

To get referrals and introductions.

SMART SELLING ACTION PLAN

The I.M.P.A.C.T approach:

- *Investigate* to generate qualified prospects.
- *Meet* with prospects to gain rapport and setup the best selling situation.
- *Probe* to discover what is wanted most and uncover real and perceived needs.
- *Apply* to show that you understand their needs and desires.
- *Convince* to prove your claims.
- *Tie it down* to negotiate a win-win agreement.

Chapter 25

Have a Plan For Schmoozing Success

To increase the success of your business or organization, take full advantage of the numerous networking opportunities available to you. Many of our clients tell us they attend various business functions, yet don't get any business from them. To turn these events to fertile opportunities of generating business and key contacts, you need a plan. At the next function, instead of pretending your fascinated by the wallpaper, try following the steps for converting functions into fortune.

Set Realistic Goals.

Prior to attending a function, determine how many contacts you want to generate from this event. Make it your objective to collect a minimal number of business card and leads. Set a realistic number. Don't go to a networking meeting thinking you are going to walk away with 100 possible names and numbers. Pick a realistic number like 15. Take the time to qualify them to make sure a follow up call is warranted.

Have Your Ten Second "Commercial" Ready.

When you meet prospects for the first time, you want to introduce yourself in a way that captures their interest right away. This is your 10-second personal commercial that explains the benefit of your product or service. If you can make it funny that's even better. Our brother Rick used to introduced himself by saying, "I sell trash." That always got their attention. Then he would go on to say that his company sold packaging materials . . . the stuff that's left over once you have the product.

Gather Information to Qualify

As you talk to these contacts, ask many open-ended questions to learn as much about their business as you can. If you learn anything important, be sure to write it on the back of their card. If you need more room write it down on a separate pad of paper you bring along. It is important you get them to talk about their business and themselves. But, don't spend too much time with anyone person. Learn the basics the move on. The more you know, the easier it will be to follow up. Be sure to get permission to follow up in the next few days.

Divide and Conquer

If you're attending a function with a coworker, don't spend time together. Don't sit at the same table. Use the time to meet new people who can potentially buy from you.

Contact Promptly

Within several days of meeting your 15 leads, be sure to follow up. This can be done by phone or a e-mail. Mention that it was great meeting them and you look forward to a beneficial business arrangement. Ask when would be a good time to get together to discuss the possibilities of working together in some way. Make it very non-threatening, but it's important to meet face to face.

Arrange A Meeting

Take the initiative to arrange a face to face meeting so you can discuss how both of your businesses can work together. Though it is possible to begin business relationships on the phone, visiting in person makes a much stronger impression. It would also to be to your advantage to first meet outside of the prospect's business. Luncheon invitations are prefect incentives to entice prospects to visit with you off site.

SMART SELLING ACTION PLAN:

- Set specific goals for the event.
- Gather information to qualify each new contact.
- Don't waste time with your colleagues.
- Follow up within several days.
- Plan to meet face to face.

Chapter 26

Getting the Sale of a Lifetime

Closing the sale of a lifetime requires a special attitude, according to Rich Gladin; a Houston based sales rep that recently bagged a $2 million sale. Gladin is a Houston based defibrillator sales rep for ZOLL Medical Corporation. After two years and surviving the sales equivalent of a "code blue" he resuscitated the sales effort, which turned out to be the largest ever in his industry. Gladin shared with us some of the key principles he feels allowed him to close this seemingly impossible deal.

1. Integrity

Prior to working for ZOLL, Gladin worked for two other medial companies for the previous 12 years. He always did his best to satisfy his customer's needs. Then when he started with ZOLL, he had a stellar reputation for making good on his promises. So, when he called on a key decision maker at the hospital about this new biphasic waveform technology developed by ZOLL, he was well received.

2. Tenacity

It takes a patience and perseverance to sell high-ticket items that have a longer buying cycle. Staying the course was critical to his ultimate success.

3. Strategic Preparation

In a sense, success was preordained due to the vision by ZOLL management. The first decision was the development and patenting of a new waveform, a type of technology that allowed ZOLL's biphasic defibrillator to perform significantly better than the two major competitor's technology. This was a "product" decision. The next was a "marketing" decision. ZOLL commissioned various independent research projects that provided conclusive scientific proof that their devise did in fact perform better for the patients than the competitors. The competition had little, if any such research to support their claims.

4. Tactical Preparation, Flexibility and Adaptability

When Gladin and his team make their presentation to the committee, they had a technical glitch. The projection system didn't work. Having presentation equipment difficulties when pitching a product can totally turn off the buyers. Fortunately the team was so well prepared and so passionate about their product, that they were still able to make a power presentation.

5. Universal Support

Though Gladin was the point person on the project, he had a team of specialists out of the corporate office, including the President of the company, willing to fly to Houston and help in dealing with all aspects of the sale.

6. Suggest Add-Ons

One interesting development after they made their presentation was an invitation to rebid, adding three additional perimeters. Think of this as adding profitable options to a basic unit. This could be looked at as the medical device equivalent of adding power windows, power seats, and a GPS that makes the basic machine more useful. These add-ons to the 180 basic units brought the original proposal of $1.2 million to $2 million.

7. Success Breeds Success

The postscript to this example is that Gladin was talking to another large hospital that competes directly with the one that just bought the new defibrillators. His contact tells him, "Well if they have them… then we have to have them too." This also looks like a sale in the $2 million range.

SMART SELLING ACTION PLAN:

- Always maintain your integrity.
- Never give up.
- Get support every where you can.
- Prepare for every contingency.
- Invest in ways to prove your claims.
- Use your success to repeat your success.

Chapter 27

Getting Religious About Prospecting

You can increase the quantity and quality of the leads and thereby increasing your sales, by following the Ten Commandments of prospecting, according to Katonah, New York, based consultant, Paul S. Goldner, author of *Red Hot Cold Call Selling, Prospecting Techniques That Pay Off!*

Commandment I: Make an appointment with yourself for one hour each day to prospect. Prospecting, like anything else, requires discipline. Prospecting is something sales people do not like to do, so it is important to set a time to prospect.

Commandment II: Make as many calls as possible to a defined target market. By doing this, you will only call the best prospects in the market.

Commandment III: Make your calls brief. The objective of the prospecting call is to get the appointment. It's difficult to sell a complex product or service over the phone. Your prospecting call should last two to three minutes and should be focused on the following:

- Introducing yourself
- Introducing your product or service
- Get a brief understanding of the prospects needs
- Provide them with a good reason to spend some of their valuable time with you

- Get a qualified appointment.

Commandment IV: Be prepared with a list of names before you call. You'll accomplish more by having at least a one month supply of names on hand at all times.

Commandment V: Work without interruption. Don't take calls and agree to attend meetings during your prospecting time. The more consistent you are with your prospecting efforts, the more appointments you'll make.

Commandment VI: Consider Prospecting during off peak hours when conventional prospecting times don't work. Some of your best prospecting will be done between 8:00 AM and 9:00 AM, between 12:00 Noon and 1:00 PM and between 5:00 PM and 6:30 PM.

Commandment VII: Vary your call times. Prospects are all creatures of habit. They are attending the same meeting each Monday at 10:00 AM. If you cannot get through at this time, call at another time.

Commandment VIII: Be organized. Use a computerized contact management system that allows you to keep notes of the call, record follow up calls, and do letters and memos. Refer to your notes when doing follow up sales calls.

Commandment IX: See the end before you begin. Dr. Steven Covey, in his book, *The Seven Habits of Highly Successful People* tells us to establish a goal and then develop a plan to work towards that goal. Your prospecting goal is to get the qualified appointment. Therefore your plan and your calling script or prompt sheet, should be designed to achieve your goal.

Commandment X: Don't stop: Persistence is one of the key virtues in selling success. Studies have shown that most sales are made after the fifth call and most sales people quit after the first.

Smart Selling Action Plan:

- Prospect for an uninterrupted hour each day.

- Have a qualified list to call from.

- Make as many calls as possible.

- Make your calls brief.

- Get organized with good notes.

- Be persistent when asking for appointments.

Chapter 28

Getting Past The Gatekeeper

(Part 1 of 2)

All your sales techniques are worthless unless you can talk with the decision maker. However in many selling situations there is a buffer or filter that keeps you from talking with the person who has the authority to make a buying decision. That obstacle could be a secretary, an assistant or some other "gatekeeper". The gatekeeper is a very dangerous person because they have the ability to say no and does not have the ability to say yes. When talking with the gatekeeper, it is important to remember to give them as little information as you can. The less they know, the better off you are.

Several Street Fighters' tactics, which allows you to sneak by the gatekeeper to the decision-maker, is best explained using a football game as an analogy. You (the sales person) is the high powered San Francisco 49er offense, the decision-maker is the goal line and the pesky gatekeeper is the defense. Here are some alternatives to help you bypass the gatekeeper.

The Run Up The Middle

This is your most direct approach and you use your "verbal" offensive line to help you break through. A good gatekeeper asks you many questions before you're allowed talk to the boss. The more questions you answer without getting "sacked" the closer your are to the goal. Respond to the question with the minimal amount of information then follow up with a request. Secretaries know that part of their job is to screen calls. Often they do not feel they have done their job suitably unless they ask some questions. They often feel that the more questions you are asked, the better they are doing their job. Therefore, the secretary often times asks you more questions despite how trivial some of those questions may be. Its only after these secretaries feel that they are doing their job properly, and assuming you gave no information that causes them to not put you through to the decision maker, do you stand a chance of getting through.

For example you might say, "This is Mitchell Nathan calling for Austin Ryan. Please put him on." Notice that it end with a *call to action*.

"And who are you with?"

"I'm with Street Fighter Inc. Please tell Mr. Ryan I'm holding for him."

"Is he expecting your call?"

"I don't believe we have set up a specific time, but please let him know I am on the line."

"And what is it regarding?"

"Let Mr. Ryan know that I have the answers to the marketing questions."

"Does he know you?"

"You know, I don't think we have met personally, but I do have that information for him so please let him know I'm holding for him."

Notice that Mitchell gave the very minimum information in answering to each of the questions. By allowing the gatekeeper to ask a lot of questions, the caller is properly screened. At the same time, Mitchell did not put the call in jeopardy by giving enough information to get disqualified.

SMART SELLING ACTION PLAN

- Make a list of the five or six most common questions gatekeepers ask you during phone calls.

- Create a brief response to each one that will not get you disqualified.

- Write out different "call to actions" to follow those responses.

- If the name of your company has a tendency to disqualify you, use an abbreviated version of it. (i.e. Slutsky Mutual Life, Inc. to Slutsky, Inc.

- Track your success rate of getting past the Gatekeepers using the "run-up-the-middle" approach.

- Never sell your product or service to the Gatekeeper. Only sell them on putting you through to the decision-maker.

Chapter 29

More On Getting Past The Gatekeeper

(Part 2 of 2)

In the previous chapter you learned that all your sales techniques are worthless unless you can talk with the decision-maker. However in many selling situations there is a buffer or filter that keeps you from talking with the person who has the authority to make a buying decision. That obstacle could be a secretary, an assistant or some other "gatekeeper". The gatekeeper is a very dangerous person because they have the ability to say no and does not have the ability to say yes. So if you can get *through* the gatekeeper, you may have to get *around* the gatekeeper.

The way you do this is not too dissimilar a football team's offense. Here are some alternatives to help you bypass the gatekeeper.

The End Run

Try reaching your prospect by calling a different department. If, for example, you want Mr. Jones in Accounts Payable, try calling shipping and ask for Mr. Jones. They'll tell you that you've reached the wrong department. Ask them to transfer you directly to Mr. Jones's office. Sometimes you'll get transferred directly into the office.

The Reverse

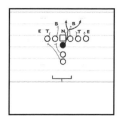

One approach that is particularly effective at times is to call the office of someone higher up in the organization. If you are trying to reach the Executive Vice President, for example, then call the Chief Executive Officer's office. The CEO's secretary will inform you that you have reached the wrong office and usually offers to transfer you to the right party. A call transferred from the boss's office stands a little better chance of getting through.

The Quarterback Sneak

Try calling very early in the morning. Often, busy executives get to the office by 6:00 or 7:00 in the morning, long before their secretaries show up. And when their phone rings there is a very good chance they will answer the phone themselves. Also try after work on weekends. This also might work at lunchtime when the Gatekeeper is gone and they put in a bench warmer.

The Bomb

The "bomb" requires that you break an earlier rule. You have tried everything and the only way you are even going to get a shot at the decision-makers is to sell the gatekeeper on the product or service. Chances for success are small but if it is the only move you have left, you have to give it your best shot.

The Punt

Sometimes you have to cut your losses. There are many more prospects out there and if you cannot get through to this one, after you have given it a good old college try, move on. You might want to throw that lead in your tickler file and give a call back in five or six months.

Smart Selling Action Plan

- 1. Review the first article on Getting Past the Gatekeeper.
- 2. This week make a commitment to make at least 50 sales telephone calls to prospective clients.

Chapter 30

Five Steps to Help You Master The Selling Dance

(Part 1 of 2)

To become a successful sales person you need more than a seminar. You need on-going training and motivation according to Bruce D'Autremont and Bob Chapman who own the Dayton and Columbus franchises of the Sandler Sales Institute. D'Autremont and Chapman stress that to be a successful sales person you need to learn a system. You need to master non-traditional sales techniques and you need to be nurtured and supported the process of learning how to sell for an extended period of time. According to Sandler dogma, to succeed in sales, you must observe only five rules:

1. Qualify your prospects.
2. Extract your prospects "pain."
3. Verify that the prospect has money.
4. Be sure the prospect is a decision-maker.
5. Match your service or product to the prospect's "pain."

When a sales person and a prospect begin what the Sandler Sales Institute calls the "selling dance" there are always two systems at work: the prospect's selling system and the sales person's selling system. The prospect's agenda is generally gathering information while giving little, negotiating for the best price and terms, and conserving time. Ideally the salesperson and the prospect should think of selling as a win-win situation. Reality is that prospects have the upper hand. To level the playing field you need to understand the steps in the "prospect's" selling system:

1. Your prospect lies to you.

Prospects lie to defend themselves. They have a preconceived idea of what to expect from a sales person. Prospects say things like "I'm not interested" when in fact, interest could be generated under more favorable conditions. The other is "I'm interested," when, in fact your prospect really isn't but is afraid of the pressure that might be applied following an honest reply.

2. Your prospect wants to know what you know.

Your prospects like to "pick your brain" because they know you bring something of value, whether it lowers costs, improves performance or saves money. Prospects want to extract all they know about your product or service and negotiate down to your best price, just to beat up their existing suppliers.

For example, we are in the business of selling speaking and training. In short, we sell information, ideas and solutions. When we're in the proposal stage of the sale we have to make sure we don't provide them a solution to their problem *before* they hire us.

3. Your prospect purposely misleads you.

Your prospect will tell you that he or she needs to think it over or will get back to you. Your prospect holds out just enough hope to make you believe you have a chance at getting the sale.

4. The prospect doesn't answer the telephone

(Or won't return your messages). This means that it's over but you don't know it. It's been over for some time but you don't want to admit it to yourself because you have invested so much in effort and time chasing what you thought was a real opportunity.

SMART SELLING ACTION PLAN:

- To avoid using your prospect's selling system instead of yours:
- You must uncover your prospect's "pain." People buy emotionally but decide intellectually. The most intense emotion is "pain."
- You must get all the money issues out on the table.
- You must discover the decision-making process your prospect uses when deciding to.
- buy or not buy a product or service.
- You must present a solution that will get rid of the prospect's pain.

Chapter 31

Don't Settle For Less

Two sisters were in the kitchen. One grabs an orange, the only one left. The second sister exclaims that she was wanted that orange. They argued about it for several minutes and then came up with a solution. They agreed to cut the orange in half. In this way each sister got at least half of what she wanted. That sounds like a fair solution to the problem, but there was one element missing from this processed information.

As it turned out, the first sister wanted the orange to create some fresh squeezed orange juice. The second sister was baking and needed the orange peel for the recipe. Had they uncovered this piece of valuable information at the beginning of their negotiations, it would have been possible for both sisters to get 100% of what they both wanted, instead of settling for half of what they wanted.

Settling for far less than you have to, in a negotiation, is one of the most common results a convenience store owner or manager can make, according to John Patrick Dolan, JD, author of *Negotiate Like The Pros.*

John suggests that before you ever get to the negotiation table, you do your homework. Gather as much information as you can about the people with whom you'll be negotiating. Here are some of the places John suggests you look for this information:

On-line

Look for articles about your vendors, advertising companies, customers or your employees. You may also find information in electronic directories like *Hoovers Handbook of American Business*. Also, look up vendors website for some company propaganda

Library

Find articles as well as other info. Most public companies, for example, will have their Annual Report on file at the library. Also look for hardcopy directories like *Who's Who*. Also search their industry trade journals.

Telephone

Be a customer and ask for brochures and background information about the company to be mailed to you. You can also do a little telephone interview.

Credit Check

Subscribe to a service like Dunn & Bradstreet and get a background check on the company. Also call the Better Business Bureau.

Public Records

There's a great deal of information available for the asking, if you ask the right people. Sometimes you may want to use the help of a professional to you get that information.

Once you begin your face-to-face negotiations, John suggestions you do more listening than talking. Ask a lot of open-ended questions. Those are the kinds that usually begin with *what, why, where, who, when*, and *how*. If you want more details about a specific topic, follow with, *"That's interesting. Tell me more."* The more you can uncover the "hidden agenda" the easier it will be for you to create a "100% win-win" situation.

Smart Selling Action Plan

13 Fatal Negotiation Mistakes You Don't Want To Make

1. Wanting something too much.

2. Believing that the other side has all of the power.

3. Failing to recognize your own strengths.

4. Getting hung up on one issue.

5. Failing to see more than one option.

6. Approaching negotiations with a win-lose mentality.

7. Short term thinking that ruins long term relationships.

8. Trying to squeeze out too much.

9. Accepting opinions, statements and feeling as facts.

10. Accepting positions as final.

11. Believing that having more authority gives you more power.

12. Talking too much and listening too little.

13. Negotiating in haste.

Chapter 32

Defusing Difficult People

There are three steps to effectively deal with difficult people according to Sandra Crowe of Pivotal Point Training & Consulting in Rockville, Maryland and author of *Since Strangling Isn't an Option.*

Step 1. Neutralize yourself

Step 2. Listen and inquire

Step 3. Move into a solution

Neutralize yourself

Difficult people often use emotions to give themselves a feeling of power. To deal with them, keep your emotions in check. Reprogram your mind or use self-talk to put yourself in the right state of mind so you don't become an emotional victim. You might tell yourself several of the following:

"I can handle myself."

"This is making me stronger."

"I am choosing my own strength."

"This isn't personal."

"I'm in control of me."

Listen and Inquire

Ask questions to find out the <u>underlying</u> problem. Engage them.

Don't pull away. Your strength comes from the engagement. At first they'll probably dispel more anger but when they're finished venting, you can more easily get to the real problem. Here are some suggestions to help you start to regain control:

"I'm sorry you feel that way."

"It wasn't my intention to hurt you."

"Let's talk about that."

"I'm confused."

"Tell me what I said or did to make your feel that way."

"Can you make this more clear?"

Move Into a Solution

This is where you deal with the underlying request. Start asking questions that give you an idea of what it would take to create a solution you both can live with. You might ask:

"Where can I start?"

"What can I do?"

"What now?"

"What's next?"

"What do you suggest?"

"Where do we go from here?"

"Let me propose this . . ."

To deal with a difficult person, Sandra suggests that you think of yourself as driving a car and the conversation is the road. You decide what road you're going to take them down. Too often the difficult person is behind the wheel and we get flustered. You need to be behind the driver's seat and lead them.

To more effectively deal with difficult people, here are three things you should try to do:

1. **Accept them:** You don't have to like them but they are human and they're probably trying to do their best.

2. **Acknowledge them:** This should be genuine. If you try to butter them up they'll probably sense it and you loose impact. Make your acknowledgment very specific.

3. **Set boundaries:** Don't let that person push you. If they're using

foul language, for example, you have to say that it is not okay. Don't let their emotional behavior zap your energy.

SMART SELLING ACTION PLAN

- Neutralize yourself when someone lashes out at you. Don't take it personally.
- Listen to what they say and inquire as to the underlying problem.
- Work to a solution as soon as possible.
- Accept them even though they may be verbally abusive to you.
- Acknowledge them but be genuine about it.
- Set boundaries. Don't put up with unacceptable behavior or language but keep your cool in the process. Don't reward the negative behavior.

Chapter 33

Dealing With The Difficult Buyer

Sales people have many different kinds of customers to sell. It is important to establish what kind of customers they are, so you know how to sell to them. Harry J. Friedman of the Friedman Group in Culver City, California and the author of *"No Thanks, I Just Looking"* classifies the customers into several categories. Here are just a few.

Marcel Marceu Type

This customer has a quiet personality and is shy to talk. As a sales person you have done everything properly, from opening the sale to probing, but little response from the customer. You ask questions about what the customer wants, and received little or no information. What's a salesperson to do?

Solution - One way to handle this type of customer is to go for the close. Trying to close the sale will initiate the customer to either buy or not buy. If the customer isn't ready to buy, then focus on asking open-ended questions to get some additional concrete information. With this additional information, then go for the close.

Monty Hall Type

This customer wants "to make a deal" on everything. He wants to buy the finest merchandise for less than your cost and is very relentless in his pursuit to get what he wants. He agrees on a price, only after you give him 50 percent off another item. When you stand firm on your offer, he insists on free delivery. What's a salesperson to do?

Solution - Let this customer know, you have gone as low as you have the authority to go. However, you're willing to make a call, if he doesn't mind waiting, to the "boss" (even if you are the boss) who can approve a larger discount. Go in the back room and make the call. Go back to the customer and say, "I told the boss you were a good customer and I would like to do better for you, but after looking up the pricing I was told I can't go less. I tried!" This customer now knows his bargaining days are over and it is time for you to close the sale.

Wishy Washy Customer

This one likes the product, can afford it, but just can't seem to say yes. Making decisions is very difficult for this customer. Every time you spend time with this customer, they leave without buying. What's a salesperson to do?

Solution - This customer can't make up their mind by themselves, so it is up to you to help. Confirm the choice by commenting on what a wise selection they have made. Mention other satisfied customers who have made a similar purchase. To help with the buying decision, write up a sales slip or delivery order. The goal is to build up the Sales

SMART SELLING ACTION PLAN

- Learn the solutions to each category so you know it well.
- Role-play the solutions with other employees until you feel comfortable.
- Identify those customers who fall into the difficult category
- Try the solutions out on customers.
- Modify the solutions if need be.

Chapter 34

Deal Only With Decision Makers Avoid Wasting Your Time

Don't waste time selling your product or service to potential clients who can't buy from you. One critical key to successful selling is to determine who is the real decision-maker. If the decision is made by more than one person, then if possible, you want to present to all the decision-makers simultaneously. Without talking to the decision maker, its infinitely more difficult to get a "yes."

Sometimes, you may find that you are forced to deal with a *decision influencer*. For example, when a national trade association is considering hiring us for a keynote or seminar at their convention, a committee often makes the final decision. Usually, we can't get direct access to that committee. So, we have to sell our program through the coordinator who takes it to the committee on our behalf. We know it is a much weaker sale because we cannot deal directly with the decision-makers.

Some salespeople ask, "Are you the decision maker?" The problem is everyone feels they are a decision-maker. But to get a more accurate response rephrase your question like this: "Other than yourself, who else would you need to consult before making the decision?" If they name someone else, then you have a good indication that you're not dealing with the key decision-maker. You now have determined the person you should be trying to deal with directly. It's all in how you phrase your question.

Sales trainer, Bill Bishop from Orlando, Florida, aptly illustrated the impact of using the proper phrasing of your questions. He told us the story of the young monk who asked the Abbot for permission to smoke his pipe when he prayed, but was turned down. He then noticed an older monk smoking a pipe. Curious now, he approached the older monk and asked how it was possible that the older monk got permission to smoke his pipe during prayers when he was turned down. The older monk took a long puff of his pipe and responded, "Well, my brother, when I approached the Abbot, I asked him an entirely different question. I asked, "if it was appropriate to pray while smoking my pipe." He informed me that *anytime was appropriate for prayer!*"

One of the most serious mistakes salespeople make is assuming they know if some is or is not a decision-maker. Several years ago, we knew a woman who was shopping for a car. She knew the type of car she wanted. She made a good living and was paying for this car herself. It was solely her decision. Yet, at the first two dealerships the salesmen refused to work with her until she brought her husband back with her. The third dealership treated her like a real customer. The salesman took her for a test drive. They negotiated the final sale. That dealership not only got that one sale, but over the next several years that same dealership got seven more sales from her relatives.

SMART SELLING ACTION PLAN

- Determine early on if you're dealing with the decision maker
- If you're dealing with a decision influencer, determine if it is possible to contact the decision-maker directly.
- If dealing with a committee, find out all you can about the committee members and their decision making process.

- Provide each committee member with original promotional materials
- Ask permission to address the entire committee or each individual committee member.
- Make no assumptions about decision-makers until you gather the information.

Chapter 35

Conditioning Yourself For Success In Sales

(Part 2 of 2)

To be successful at sales you must condition yourself in much the same way as an athlete, doctor, professor or any good professional according to Growth Resources of Ohio, Ltd. a Sandler Sales Institute. They've documented that those who become and stay top performers condition themselves daily for success. Bruce D'Autremont and Bob Chapman, who own the Sandler Sales Institute franchises in Dayton and Columbus, suggested ten rules to help you.

1. **Stay on the right side of the trouble line.** Sales people get themselves in trouble when they spend too much on "no pay time." Top sales people always know the difference between "pay time" and "no pay time."

2. **Burn your bridges**. You know it's not easy to make a living selling. Don't tell yourself that if things don't work out you can always fall back on your old profession. Once you do that you've lost the battle.

3. **Get mentally and emotionally tough.** Failure is part of the process of becoming successful. You'll get a lot of "no's". Top performers know that they can learn from their failures.

4. **Maintain a healthy self-esteem.** Everyone wants to feel good,

but some people can only feel good at the expense of others. People with a poor self-image can't feel good about themselves, so they'll frequently attack anyone who has a better self-image. Sales people make easy targets. By not taking it personally you're avoiding feeling bad about yourself.

5. **Cultivate a support group.** If you want to be a top performer, find other top performers and those who want to be. Just make sure you don't spend this time on the wrong side of the "trouble line."

For example, when our clients hire us to train their managers (or franchisees, agents, etc.) we get them together once a month for a meeting. Each participant gets an opportunity to share his or her successes with the group as well as ask the group for help in problem areas. If one person is having a certain challenge in his or her territory, the others often come to their rescue with ideas and words of encouragement.

6. **Know when to use product knowledge.** It's important for you to know as much as possible about your product or service but the same is not always true for your prospect, especially during the initial sales call.

7. **Know your competition.** Spend time going to the competition's seminars, reading their brochures, and learning their strengths and weaknesses.

8. **Keep a journal.** Top performers set daily goals. Goal setting helps them take control of every day.

9. Work a prospecting system. Top performers spend 80 percent of their time servicing their clients and customers and only 20 percent of their time prospecting. Top sales people get their clients and customers to prospect for them.

10. **Use a system for selling.** Your sales system must include both an emphasis on self-esteem (correct behavior) as well as an emphasis on technique training. To get to the top you have to practice repeatedly. Spend time getting to know your system to the point where you "own" the system.

SMART SELLING ACTION PLAN:

- Identify the hours during your day that are key selling times for you.

- Commit to spending that time for selling and move other activities outside that time.

- Look for people who are supportive in your efforts to achieve your sales goals.

- Once you find your support group, meet on a regular basis (at least monthly).

- This week commit to finding out something new about your competition.

- Start keeping a daily journal about your sales activities.

-

Chapter 36

Lose More Sales By Knowing Emotional Boundaries

One way to get better results when you're selling is *not* by espousing tons of product knowledge. On the contrary, you may discover that your prospect's or client's are more receptive with you first ask their permission to share your information with them, according to Linda Talley, author of *Business Finesse: Dealing With Sticky Situations in the Workplace for Managers*.

It's about having emotional boundaries

Which most people don't have or honor. If you are the one that is honoring you're client's emotional as well as physical boundaries, they will be more attracted to doing business with you."

We honor physical boundaries such as closed or locked doors, but how often do we honor the emotional boundary? Rarely, especially if we want the customer to do something for us - such as BUY. As a salesperson, you may be three steps ahead of the client but if you don't come back to be with that customer in the present moment, to honor them, you're going to lose them. They won't feel comfortable with you.

Highly Trained Professionals

Most sales people are highly trained professionals and have lots of information and knowledge to give to the customer. Most people have a tendency to *vomit* this information on the customer without asking if that's OK. And usually, that's not OK.

The customer wasn't ready and so they feel uncomfortable - violated. You did not condition the conversation by asking permission.

Conditioning the Conversation

When you ask permission to have the conversation, you honor the other person's boundaries. They will give you a *yes* or *no* answer. When they respond with a yes, they are ready to have a conversation. Until you condition the conversation, you can say anything you want and they may or may not hear it. When they don't hear it and you say it, you have to repeat yourself. This is not very productive and very irritating to you. For example: A customer asks you when you can deliver a specific product. You may want to jump in there and say, "First thing next week." Instead, ask permission by saying, "May I tell you?" Get a *yes* or *no* from your customer because when they say yes, that's a key buying signal and you won't be wasting your time. Whenever you have information to give a customer, ask permission. If they don't give it, go back and ask again but don't give your information till you have permission.

Smart Selling Action Plan

Begin by practicing this skill at home or in the office - some place that feels safe to try out new sales skills.

- Share this skill with other members of your organization. See how productivity picks up.
- People want information - you want a relationship if you are going to get the sale. Make certain that you have the relationship by asking for more than enough permission.
- Whenever a customer asks a question, ask permission to tell them before you give the information.

- Always get a *yes* or *no* from your customer. If it's *no* you've saved yourself a lot of time.

- Ask for more than enough permission. If you ask and they don't say *yes* or *no*, keep asking till you get an answer. Retrain your customer to want to hear what you have to say.

Chapter 37

Clever Phone Numbers Help Ring Your Bell

Words are worth a thousand phone numbers. Spelling out a key work will make it easier for your customers and prospects to remember your number. For example, advertisements for ABLE Roofing feature their number, 444-ROOF. Atlas Butler Heating and Cooling likewise feature their number: 800-FURNACE. Nationally, companies including 800-FLOWERS and 800-MATTRESS not only made the number memorable; they named their company after their number. Another great example is Hooked On Phonics: 800-A-B-C-D-E-F-G. Not to be out done, we also decided to take advantage of this clever marketing tool by securing 800-SLUTSKY. Nobody else wanted that number so we grabbed it!

When you're looking to get a memorable phone number for your business, here are few tips to help you leverage this valuable marketing tool:

Incorporate it in all of your advertising. Include this number in all your advertising, letterhead, on vehicles, and everywhere your company name appears. Think of it as an extension of your company name.

Make sure you buy similar numbers. With all vanity numbers, there can be confusion converting letters to number. If available, secure similar numbers or numbers that is frequently mis-dialed to reach you. Able Roof not only has 444-ROOF, but also, 444-ABLE and 444-7003. Why the last one? Because people, sometimes misread the "O" for a zero. Before they bought the 7003 number, they were losing around 300 calls per month. With our number, we reserved it with the last digit as a "4" instead of a "9" because people often spell "Slutsk<u>Y</u>" as "Slutsk<u>I</u>".

Incorporate your number as your URL address. If you already have a memorable number turn it into an address on the Web." This has been done very successfully, for example, with WWW.800FLOWERS. COM. I use 800slutsky@gmail.com.

Spell out the number. While a pneumonic number is memorable, the caller still must convert the letters to number. Make it easy for them. After your *word number*, in parentheses, Italics, or a smaller typeface, place the numerical version. We do this in all our promotional pieces: 800-SLUTSKY (*800-758-8759*). However, if your ad or letter is asking for an immediate phone call, place the numerical number first, followed by the word number. Get creative when looking for a memorable number. For local number it's best to use a four-letter word, unless the exchange spells out your word perfectly. On toll free numbers, you want to use seven letter words. Write down a number of four-letter and seven-letter words that describe your business. Then see if those numbers are available. Perhaps 800-SHINGLE would also be a good number for a roofing company or a doctor treating the condition by the same name. Local numbers that spell HEAT or COOL might be great for an HVAC company. A plumber or even an urologist could use a number ending in 5325 (LEAK). There are a lot of possibilities.

If possible, avoid words with the letters "O", "I", or "L". These two letters could easily be confused with "zero" and "one". The letter "L" can also sometimes be confused with the number "one".

SMART SELLING ACTION PLAN:

Tips on getting the most from vanity phone numbers:
- Use the vanity number in all your advertising, correspondence and forms..
- Follow the *word number* with numerical version for easy

dialing.

- Secure other numbers that customers might confuse as yours including the most frequently mis-dialed numbers.
- Try to get both a local version and a toll free version.
- Use the word number as part of your web address.

Business Cards Can Connect You To More Customer

You can easily turn a simple, inexpensive business card into a powerful marketing too. All you have to do is, two to three times a day, hand out your card to someone who is not your customer or client. Start with people you already come in contact with. When you're running errands, for example, you're likely to come in contact with the waiter at the local restaurant, the grocery store clerk, hair stylist, your mail person, the dry cleaner clerk, the check out person at the discount store, and even the police officer giving you a warning to slow down. The list is endless. Simply hand them your business card then introduce yourself and invite them to become your customers or client.

Free Cup of Coffee Creates New Customers

Barbara is the manager of a convenience store in Parkersburg, West Virginia. During an eleven week period, she passed out 200 of her business cards to people she did not recognize as being her customers. On the back of her business card she would write "free regular soft drink or coffee" and sign it. Then she would tell them that when they come into her convenience store, the soft drink was on her. Of the 200 she passed out 51 came back for over a 25% return. Obviously most of those who came in and redeemed that card, bought other things. Plus, many of those customers came back for more visits.

Hindsight Promotion

A very successful stockbroker on the East Coast used a different version of business card distribution according to, author of *The Great Brain Robbery*. While commuting to work, this stockbroker would have to pay several tolls. Before he would pay his tolls, he would first look in his rear view mirror. If he would see an upscale car, he not only would pay his toll but also pay the toll of the person in the luxury car behind him. He then asked the toll booth attendant to hand his business card to the person in the car behind him after writing a brief note on the back of the card. The note read, "If you think this is an interesting way of getting your attention, think of all the things I could do for your financial portfolio." He got many new clients from a simple 90¢ toll and a clever use of his business card.

SMART SELLING ACTION PLAN

- Get 1000 business cards printed.
- Pass out at least 20 business cards each week to potential new customers or clients.
- As you pass out your business card, introduce yourself and ask them to become your customer.
- If appropriate to your business, offer an incentive. Hand write the offer (a discount, value added, or small free offer) on the back of the card that encourages them to try you the first time.
- Track your results to see how many come back for another visit.
- When your 1000 business cards are gone, print another 1000.

Chapter 39

Asking The Prospect Why They Won't Buy Might Save The Sale

Did you ever have a sale that you were 99.9 percent sure was going to close, just fall apart? It's a common tale for many sales people. The reason it fell apart was because the client or customer had a hidden objection or there was an unresolved issue or concern. Since that issue was not addressed, it led to the dissolution of a sale. And since that prospect makes a decision, albeit the wrong one, it makes it extremely difficult to work your way back in. What you need is a technique that allows you to uncover those hidden objections before you ask for the order.

The technique we are about to suggest is one that scares many sales people. The reason it's scary is that you are going to ask for a negative response from your prospect. Here's how it works: You're almost positive that the prospect is ready to buy. Just before you close, ask one more questions,

"You know, based on all the information we've shared and everything we've discussed, *what's the one thing that would keep us from getting a go-ahead* right now?"

This question, which you would obviously tailor to your own situation, assumes that there is an objection. You are actually encouraging that prospect to come up with a reason *not* to buy! The question specifically asks, "what the one reason," not "is there any reason." However, the reason that this approach can help save many sales for you is this: The objection was there anyway. That prospect may have been concerned about the price, the specs, the delivery date, the service and any number of other items. The concerns are there. This question merely brings them to the surface so you have one last opportunity to deal with those items before you lose the sale. If those concerns aren't dealt with at this point in the sale, it more than likely will come back and haunt you later on with a cancellation.

Of course, the other possible response to the question is, "no reason," in which case you can assume the sale is final. Also, notice some of the words used in this question. Instead of saying some like, "sign the contract" we suggest you use a less threatening term like, "get the go-ahead, get the ball rolling or give it a try."

Then, once you deal with that hidden objection, you ask the question again, and keep asking it until you've get a response that tells you there is nothing standing between you and the confirmation of the sale.

It's scary at first, but give it a try (non-threatening term.). We think you will see a significant difference in your close ration and a reduction in cancellations.

SMART SELLING ACTION PLAN

- Make a list of all the sales for the past month that you felt you had but fell through.

- Try to recall the reasons they fell through and write them down.

- Modify the "what's the one thing" question to work with selling your product or service.

- For the next month, use the "what's the one thing" approach for those sales you feel are sure to close.

- Compare your close ratio before and after the technique.

Chapter 40

12 Reasons Why Salespeople Fail

(Part 1 of 2)

There are a dozen key reasons why salespeople fail according to Sylvia Allen of Allen Consulting in Holmdel, New Jersey. She is the coauthor of *How to Be Successful at Sponsorship Sales.* While her program is geared to people who sell sponsorships, we feel that she offers many suggestions that salespeople in practically any area can get more results.

1. Not Making Enough Calls.

You can't close people you don't call on. Remember, your competition is happy to make the extra effort.

2. Not Following Through With Promises Made.

Prospects judge you by what you do, not by what you say. Be conservative with your promises and liberal with delivering on your promises.

3. Not Listening.

Your understanding of your prospect's unique needs will not increase by talking. Listen twice as hard and talk half as much and you'll double your sales.

4. Not Starting Every Day With A Plan.

Set goals for each day and each week. NASA did not land on the moon by accident. To coin a cliché, "If you fail to plan, you plan to fail."

5. Not describing Customer Benefits Clearly, Succinctly and Persuasively.

Prospects are persuaded by "meaty" words, not "watery" sentences. Good presentations are short and the results of long preparation. A poor sales presentation is usually due to minimal time spent on preparation.

6. Not Asking For The Order Often Enough.

Failing to ask for the order is the same as asking for failure. Few customers buy on the first closing attempt. Successful salespeople ask for the order several times on each call.

7. Negatively Prejudging the Prospect's Ability To Buy.

If you imagine that your prospect won't buy, you're developing a self-fulfilling prophecy. Ask questions and check the facts before even thinking of discounting the sale or offering additional concessions.

8. Not Dealing With Customer Objections Head-On.

When a prospect has an objection, welcome it as question that you're happy to answer. Objections are often buying signals in disguise.

9. Ignoring The Power of a Positive Attitude.

When things don't go your way, change your attitude. A positive attitude will help you cope with failure, rejection and disappointment.

10. Not Changing and Growing.

Welcome change as your friend. Granted, change and growth bring pain, but resisting change and growth lead to more failure and greater pain.

11. Lack Of Focus On Priorities.

Salespeople with a clear focus on the most important and most urgent takes will always get better results and than salespeople who allow themselves to get side-tracked.

12. Failure To Work Harder and Smarter.

People who are willing to work harder and smarter will win global competition. Sales people who quit early will be asked to leave sooner.

Smart Selling Action Plan:

- Review the dozen reasons why salespeople fail.
- Select one of the twelve points that you feel MOST applies to you.
- On a piece of paper, list three to five specific steps you can take to improve in that area.
- Focus for one week on improving that one point.
- Repeat the process for the next point that MOST applies to you.
- Continue this process until all twelve points have been addressed.

Chapter 41

Voice Mail Messages That Get Returned

Voice Mail can be one of the most frustrating developments for sales people because it makes it almost impossible to get through to your prospect. However, according to Orval Ray Wilson, coauthor of *Guerrilla Tele-Selling*, there are some creative ways you can entice your prospect to return your voice mail message. We find that when we leave a standard message on voice mail that we'll get half of our messages returned.

The Insomnia Message

Since most voice mail has a time stamp, you can leave messages at odd hours to make a strong impression. "Hi, it's Mitchell Austin calling. It's 3:30 in the morning and I was just thinking about your account with us, and I couldn't sleep, so I decided to leave you this message . . ."

The Mile-High Message

Next time you're on a plane, use the onboard phone call people that you wish to reach. "Hi, it's Amanda Justin. I'm calling from 37,000 feet on my way to Chicago. I was thinking about you and just had to call." According to Orval Ray, it's well worth the high price to leave an impression. If they're in the office, tell the secretary that you're calling from the plane, and you'll probably put right through.

The Stock Holder's Message

Buy a few shares of your prospect's stock. Then leave a message introducing yourself as a concerned stockholder.

The "Who You're NOT" Message

"Hi. I'm not with the IRS; I'm not selling insurance, I'm not looking for a job or donation, I don't want to borrow money, but I do want to talk to you about . . ."

The "Disregard That Message" Message

The first message you leave is, "Hi Char. Please disregard that last message. If you need anything else, please call me at . . . "Last message? What last message?

The File A Missing Person Report Message

"Hello Ron. Your staff doesn't seem to know where you are and frankly I'm concerned. I just wanted to let you know that I've filed a missing person report."

The Persistent or Pest Message

Larry Winget, a motivational speaker based out of Scottsdale, AZ uses this one: "There's a fine line between being persistent and being a pest. I want to serve you well, yet never be a pest. Will you please call and tell me how best to serve you?"

The Kiddy Call Message

Have your kids make a call. "My daddy is going crazy waiting for you to call him back. Would you please call? As soon as you do, he can take me for ice cream."

Smart Selling Action Plan

- This week, each time you get voice mail, try a different message form this article.
- Be sure to write down which message you left for each voice mail contact.
- Track the number of returned phone calls you get for each type of message you left.
- Once you start to see a particular message working, start using it more often.
- When you think of your own creative message to use, give it a try and track the results.
- Caution: there's a fine line between creativity and deception.

Chapter 42

The Powers Of Questions

(Part 1 of 3)

The right questions can help you move forward, and get you through the rough times according to Dorothy Leads, a New York City based speaker, trainer and author of *The 7 Powers of Questions: Secrets to Successful Communications in Your Life and Work*. Better questions provide better answers, and better answers give you better solutions. Dorothy suggests that if you improve your questions, you will improve your relationships at home and work.

Dorothy conducted extensive research over the past twenty years on questions and their role in communication. She has found that questions hold seven very specific powers:

Questions demand answers

When someone asks you a question, you are compelled to answer it. This feeling of obligation is what Dorothy refers to as the "answering reflex."

Questions stimulate thinking

When someone asks a question, it stimulates thinking in both the person asking and the person being asked.

Questions give you valuable information

Asking the right question can give us the specific and relevant information we want and need.

For example, we were negotiating a consulting and training contract with a restaurant chain with over forty units. To do the work right and get them results, we knew we would have to ask for a fairly high retainer fee, over one year, so we could afford to put the effort in the project that it needed. Our concern was that the client would try to reduce the monthly retainer, thus reducing the intensity of the effort we could provide them. So we asked the following questions, "What's the one thing that would keep us from getting approval on this program today?" As a result we learned that the monthly retainer fee was not a problem at all. Their main concern was having the option of discontinuing the program after six months if they felt they're weren't getting the results. Since we are supremely confident in our abilities to improve their sales, we whole-heartedly agreed.

Questions get people to open up

There is nothing more flattering than being asked to tell your personal story, or to give your opinions, insights and advice. Asking questions shows others that you are interested in who they are and what they have to say, and when that happens, even the most reticent individuals are willing to share their thoughts and feelings.

Getting people to open up can be particularly helpful to managers. Instead of giving your employees or vendors solutions to problems, encourage them to think about their own solutions. Ask questions like, "What do you feel are your options here?" "If you proceed in that direction, what are the possible results?" Psychologist Beth Althofer said, "Questions necessarily provoke thought, at least if they are good questions. If we hesitate to answer, barring privacy or personal reasons, usually it is because we recognize the complexity of the possible answers."

SMART MARKETING ACTION PLAN:

- Use questions to compel someone to answer you.
- Use questions to stimulate thinking.
- Use questions to uncover valuable information.
- Use questions to get people to open up.
- Use questions to get employees to develop their own solutions to problems.

Chapter 43

More Powers Of Questions

(Part 2 of 3)

Questions are the communication tool for the 21st Century according to Dorothy Leads, a New York City based speaker, trainer and author of the soon to be released The 7 Powers of Questions: Secrets to Successful Communications in Your Life and Work.

Questions put you in control

Everyone feels most comfortable and confident when he or she is in control. Because questions demand answer, the power goes to the asker.

Questions improve your listening skills

As you improve the art and skill of asking the right question, the answers you get become more pertinent and focused, making it easier for you to concentrate on what's important to the situation.

Questions help people to persuade themselves

People believe that what they say, not what you say. They are more likely to believe something they "thought up," and a well-phrased question can get their minds headed in a specific direction. The question is the most overlooked tool in the art of persuasion.

Barriers to asking more questions

If questions are such a powerful tool, why don't people make better use of them? Dorothy has compiled a list of reason:

- Fear of questioning authority.
- Concerns that asking questions puts us in a submissive position.
- Fear of looking stupid.
- Thinking that asking questions is rude.
- Never learning how.

In her autobiography, Barbara Bush: *A Memoir, the former First Lady* describes how after much thought she finally realized that her issue should be literacy - that everything would be better "if more people could read, write and comprehend. So the campaign was told that literacy was my interest - but we forget to mention that I knew absolutely nothing about the subject, at least not yet." One day, on a campaign stop, she was led into a meeting where her hostess said, "We are so excited about your visit. I have collected literacy experts from all around Milwaukee, some forty-five of the most informed people …we can't wait to hear what you have to say."

"I was lucky," writes Mrs. Bush, "for it suddenly came to me what to do. After saying a very few words, I asked them a question: 'If you were married to he President and had the opportunity to really make a dent in the field of illiteracy, what one thing would you do? How would you go about it?'" Needless to say, the room came alive with excellent suggestions.

"I certainly did learn something there, " she concludes. "People would rather hear themselves talk than someone else. So when in doubt, keep quiet, listen, and let others talk. They'll be happy, and you might learn something."

Hot Potato

One of the "Street Fighter Marketing" techniques we use in our seminar to get people used to asking questions is a fun exercise called "hot potato." At your next sales meeting, pair everyone off. Select a fun subject you can easily talk about for five minutes. (i.e. vacations, food, movies, etc.) The first person must ask a question about that subject. Once the question is asked, the second person now has the "hot potato." The only way to give it back is to first, answer the question as briefly as possible. Then follow up with your own question. The first person who forgets to end with a question, loses.

Smart Marketing Action Plan:

- Use questions to put you in control.
- Use questions to improve your listening skills.
- Use questions to help you persuade yourselves.
- Do the "hot potato" exercise at your next meeting.
- More info write: Dorothy Leeds, 800 West End Ave. NY, NY 10025

Chapter 44

Examples of Powerful Questions

(Part 3 of 3)

Questions are the key to communication according to Dorothy Leads, a New York City based speaker, trainer and author of *The 7 Powers of Questions: Secrets to Successful Communications in Your Life and Work*. In this last of the three-part series, samples and thought starters of questions are listed. Select the ones most appropriate for your situation:

Getting to the specifics.

These questions are meant to help you clarify, define, probe and get to the bottom of issues and circumstances. The key is to ask these questions in a non aggressive manner so people don't get defensive or annoyed.

- Can you clarify that?
- Can you give me an example of what you mean?
- What specifically do you mean by that?
- Do you have any questions about what I just said?
- What specific results are you looking for?
- What do you plan to do with this information, report, project?
- What is the real problem here?

- Tuning in to others. Part of understanding another person is to be tuned into his or her emotional state or way of thinking.
- From what standpoint are you asking?
- How do you feel about it?
- How strongly do you feel about it?
- What's most important to you?
- What are your priorities?
- If I were in [his or her] shoes, how might I be feeling?
- Tuning in to yourself:
- How do I feel about it?
- What do I think about it?
- What is my purpose?
- What assumptions am I making?
- What am I really trying to say with my message?
- What is the best way to phrase this question?
- Getting feedback from others. To get feedback, be prepared to ask clarifying questions. The more specific you want the feedback to be, the more specific your question must be.
- Did I understand you correctly what you said?
- Did I answer your question?
- How am I doing?
- Have I done what you requested?
- Giving feedback to others:
- What type of feedback would be most helpful to you?
- What do you plan to do with the feedback?
- Do you want me to just listen?
- Do you want me to ask questions and interact with you?
- Do you want me to give you advice?
- Closing. To find where the person stands, ask a closing question.
- Are you ready to go ahead?
- Is it a deal?
- Consequences:
- Is it worth it?
- What will I regret not doing?
- What might the short-term results be?
- What might the long-term results be?

- Personal: These questions are limitless. The easiest way to get into the asking habit is to begin by asking yourself questions.
- Can you help me?
- Can I help you?
- Am I where I want to be?
- What do I want to do?
- Where do I want to spend the rest of my life?
- What are my options?
- What questions should I be asking?
- What do I need to do to meet my goals?
- What am I willing to change to get there?
- What did I accomplish?
- What could have I done better?
- What should I ask?

Biz Smart Action Plan:

- Review the questions above.
- Select the ones that make the most sense to you.
- More info write: Dorothy Leeds, 800 West End Ave. NY, NY 10025

Chapter 45

Top Ten Telephone Basics

Good telephone skills are essential for your business to stay successful. Shep Hyken, a professional speaker in St. Louis and author of the
popular customer service book, *Moments of Magic* says these skills
are for everyone in your company from a receptionist to a warehouse
manager to a CEO. Having good telephone skills helps build stronger
relationships with everyone! Whether the call is incoming or outbound,
Hyken suggests the following to be applied to every call.

Top Ten Telephone Basics

Good telephone skills are essential for your business to stay successful. Shep Hyken, a professional speaker in St. Louis and author of the
popular customer service book, Moments of Magic says these skills
are for everyone in your company from a receptionist to a warehouse
manager to a CEO. Having good telephone skills helps build stronger
relationships with everyone! Whether the call is incoming or outbound,
Hyken suggests the following to be applied to every call:

1. Enthusiasm. Try to convey some type of enthusiasm. From beginning to end, show that you care about the person you are talking to.
Have a positive attitude. It is contagious.

2. Smile. Even though you are on the phone, the other person can sense
a smile from you. Telephone experts recommend putting a mirror on

your desk to remind you when you are not smiling at the customer.

3. Voice. Using the right tone of voice creates atmosphere on the phone. Your tone and voice inflections will create an impression and help the person on the other end understand what you are telling them.

4. Say "Hello!" (or good morning, good afternoon, etc.) Have a warm greeting or opening. Welcome people into the conversation. Don't make them feel as if they are an interruption.

5. Say "Goodbye." Have a strong closing. At the minimum, be sure to say goodbye before hanging up the phone. How many times have you expected someone to say goodbye, have a nice day, etc. only to hear a click? Don't do that to your customer!

6. Talk Simple. When talking to a customer, avoid company or technical terminology they may not understand. Technical terms or industry buzz-words can put a customer in an uncomfortable position. They might feel dumb because they don't understand you. Or, they may feel frustrated and become impatient.

7. Stay Calm. Don't get angry, even if the customer is. If a customer is complaining and angry, let them vent. Most likely they aren't mad at you personally. Ask them questions to show that you care. Don't add to their aggravation. Be a good listener.

8. Transfer ONLY ONCE! If you are transferring to someone else, make sure that person is available. Don't put the customer on the hold, transfer, hold, transfer, hold, transfer, routine.

9. Control the "hold" button. A survey in USA Today conducted by Nancy Friedman (a.k.a. The Telephone Doctor) showed that customers hate to be put on HOLD! There are really only two reasons to put someone on hold: to transfer to someone else or to get information.

10. More on controlling that "hold" button. If you are going to make a customer wait on hold, for any reason, let them know how long they will have to wait. If the customer is going to be on hold for an extended period of time, call them back at a specific time. Then, keep your promise! By following these simple 10 steps, you will bring a calm feeling to your customers and client when they call in or you call them.

Smart Selling Action Plan.

- Train your employees the proper way to answer the phone and check up on them periodically.
- Always smile and be enthusiastic when you answer the phone or call a client.
- Greet each customer with a hello and a proper goodbye.
- When you talk with an angry customer be sure to stay calm.
- Try not to leave a customer on hold for very long.

Chapter 46

Advantages and Pitfalls of Being A Specialist

You can increase your success by decreasing your market by carving out a niche. This allows you to position yourself as a specialist in that area, which provides you three big advantages:

1. Client Perception

When a person has a problem they often think that his or her situation is unique. To handle his or her problem properly takes special care and expertise. In reality this may or not be true. Still, the client perception is that it is true. The "perceived" value of your services is all that really matters when a client chooses the person to solve a problem.

2. Expertise Level

When you focus your business into a few specialized areas, you allow yourself the ability to master those particular areas in ways that a generalist can't. No doubt your profession or business is becoming more complex and will continue to do so. By specializing you are making it easier on yourself to stay abreast of the latest developments in your specific specialty area. You may not and probably could not do this in all the different services provided by a generalist.

126

You can be a specialist and still provide full service to your clients. In larger organizations individuals have their own different specialties but the whole of the organization provides the client with any service that may be required. In smaller groups you can ally yourself with other noncompetitive specialists.

3. Fee and price integrity

This is connected to your expertise level. A specialist is perceived as having more knowledge in a very specific narrow area. Consequently, most clients who have great need of this expertise are willing to pay a premium for it. Not only will they pay a premium but they'll feel better about it.

Despite all of the advantages of being a specialist there are four dangers you need to consider when looking into your specialization.

Danger #1: Market Limitations

When choosing a specialty or a few specialties there's always a risk of creating too narrow of a market. Make sure there's a big enough potential to make your specialization worth your while.

Danger #2: Seasonal Swings

If the industry in which you've dominated has big seasonal swings, you may find that your business does too. To smooth out the peaks and valleys you might look into specializing in a second or third industry with opposite seasons.

Danger #3: Cyclical Swings

Specializing in industries with big down turns can pose even more of a danger than seasonal industries. You usually don't know when you're headed into a major down turn or how long it's going to last. The solution is similar to seasonal businesses. Choose other specialties that have opposite cycles. For example, when conventions get soft, so does the demand for keynote speakers. To counter, we also offer consulting and in-depth sales and marketing projects which usually pick up when the speaking starts to drop.

Danger #4: Geographical disadvantage.

Specialization may require that your expand "geographically." You may find that your current territory does not have enough clients in your "demographic" territory. So, though you may be getting higher fees and prices, you may have to do some extra traveling to work with your targeted client base.

BizSmart Action Plan:

- Select a market niche in which you feel you can dominate.
- Select your niche based on your skills and knowledge in that area. Consider adding a second niche that smooths out seasonal and cyclical soft periods.
- The more narrow your niche, the broader you'll have to market, geographically.
- Reinforce your position as the "expert" in this niche in all your marketing efforts.

Chapter 47

How To Work a Room for Sales Success

Talking to strangers is a big fear for many. Successful sales people must do it all the time, according to Susan RoAne, a San Francisco-based keynote speaker, coach and best-selling author of *How to Work a Room, the Secrets of Savvy Networking* and *What Do I Say Next?*

In order to be an effective sales professional, you are expected to work the room for business leads, contacts, alliances and customers. What stops us, RoAne told us, is that 93 percent of adults self-identify as shy and that means most of the people we encounter at conventions, events, meetings and parties are NOT comfortable being there.

There are three roadblocks that most of us learned when we where children that keep us from being effective sales people in social situations. Fortunately, there are remedies for each that we can utilize to enhance our confidence and comfort in any room.

Roadblock #1: Don't talk to Strangers.

That may be great advice in some situations, in some areas of town but just does not make sense at a client's holiday party, an industry event, a local Chamber meeting or fundraiser.

The Remedy: Redefine the term stranger.

Whenever you are with colleagues, potential customers or our personal networks, there is a commonality. People do business with people they know, like and trust. Before you go anywhere, take a few minutes to think of who may be at that event, party or meeting and what you have in common with the other attendees.

Roadblock #2: Wait for a proper introduction.

You were likely taught that you should only talk to those to whom you've been properly introduced.

The Remedy: Have a planned, practiced self introduction.

That introduction should be under ten seconds long and keyed to the specific event. How you introduce yourself at a local business function may be very different than at your niece's graduation.

At a business function, it is best that we give the BENEFIT of what we do, rather than the title, according to Patricia Fripp, keynote speaker . "When one gives the benefit, it allows the other person to be engaged by asking a question or making a comment and the conversation begins."

The best salespeople are those who have conversations with customers and potential customers. They do not have to worry about which sales technique they are using... because the conversation builds rapport and comfort. People do business with people they know, like and trust...and around whom they are comfortable.

Roadblock #3: Good Things Come o Those Who Wait.

Instead use the RoAne version: "good things come to those who *initiate.*" If you don't say anything and WAIT, nothing will happen.

The remedy: Act like the host, not the guest.

Hosts see that others are comfortable, they are welcomed and that they are introduced in a manner that is enthusiastic and respectful and inspires conversation among the newly- introduced.

More RoAne Tips:

Save the sales pitches for a followup meeting or call. There are some sales trainers who espouse the 'do a needs assessment' philosophy of attending events. It could work in some instances but conversation is an exchange.

How to Deal With Forgotten Names.

1. Always offer your handshake and say your name. Most people respond in kind and will say their name. Then no one struggles with the forgotten name.

2. Tell the truth. "OH it has been just one of those days. So sorry I forgot, But could you help me out and tell me your name?" We all have those days and forget even our own names and people are forgiving when we are vulnerable.

Name Tag Tip: Always wear your name tag on the right hand side as that is the line of sight when shaking hands.

BizSmart Action Plan:

- Effective selling at social events:
- You initiate your own introduction
- Have a prepared introduction that's under ten seconds
- Think of things you'll have in common with the attendees
- Think more like a "host" instead of a "guest"
- Don't "sell," but rather establish contacts and rapport
- If you forget a name, be honest and ask for it.

Chapter 48

Getting what you want using the "echo"

Getting what you want requires that you to have the ability to convince someone that the value of your idea, product, or service is worthy of their commitment. The communication process that you use to get a commitment is basically the same regardless of application: negotiating important concessions from suppliers, getting new clients to become members of your barter company, getting your members to spend more of their barter dollars or expanding services from existing ones, or even getting your spouse to agree to watch a certain TV show. It boils down to one idea that most people know but have forgotten:

The person asking the questions is in control of the conversation and you have to be in control of the conversation before you can get what you want.

Most people have a tendency to talk too much and listen too little, yet by reversing this common practice you have a great advantage in any conversation that allows you to discover what it's going to take to get that person to agree with your point of view. To illustrate consider the following very unhappy experience I had while shopping for a new car:

The odd thing was that after the experience I discovered I was not alone. At the time I was driving a big luxury car and thought it was time to buy a sports car. A close friend of mine had a very nice sports car and let me drive it a couple times. I soon decided that the one thing I wanted most out of life was to drive fast and look like cool.

I started shopping around at a number of dealerships and every time the same thing happened. Some guy in a plaid polyester sport coat comes out, shakes my hand, pops the hood on the car to show me the engine and then starts talking about how much money he can save me. There I am, starring underneath the hood of these cars. I have no idea how an engine works. I look at all these tubes, and wires and fans and belts and it means absolutely nothing to me. The salesman is going on and on and cams and liters and ratios and this and that. I have no idea what he is talking about. All I want is to drive fast and look like cool.

Finally at one of the places I went to a salesman comes out while I am looking over a certain particular car. It was hot. But captured my attention was that he did not pop the hood. Instead he asked me a question, "I see you're interested in one of our most popular cars. Let me ask you, what is it about this car that grabbed your attention?"

He was showing interest in me. I got a little excited and responded, "My buddy has one very similar to this and he let me drive it. I couldn't believe how fast it was and how well it handled."

"You like to drive fast?"

"Oh yea."

"I had this one out the other day and cranked it up to 110!"

"Wow"

"And then I shifted into second!"

"WOW!"

"Not only that, whenever I took the car out, everybody thought I was cool."

"I'll take it!"

He had me. I sold me what I wanted. He found out my hot buttons. I looked at numerous comparable cars for weeks, but no one offered the solution to my problem, drive fast and look like a big shot. Even so he would not sell me that car. I could not believe it. Instead he comes back with, "listen. You do not want this car and I will tell you why.

For $3000 more I can get you a sticker on the back that says, 'turbo.'"

"What's it do?"

"I don't really know, but you can drive faster and you'll look cooler!"

"I'll take it!"

And he was absolutely right. Everywhere I went everyone notice the little turbo sticker. I thought turbo was a type of fish. I did not know. But he knew what I wanted to buy and sold it me. And I felt great about my decision. I knew that this car, with turbo, is what I really wanted all along.

Asking questions, not pitching or selling features, is the way to uncover the real needs and problems, which in turn allows you to offer your solution and get the commitment to either join your barter company or spend their barter dollars.

Staying In Control With The Echo -- One way to stay in control of the conversation and, at the same time, gain a lot of valuable information is to use a technique called the "echo." We first learned this from Bill Bishop a number of years ago and it really works great. The idea originally came from psychotherapists. If you have ever been to one you may have noticed that they always answer a question with a question.

"Well Doc, do you think I'm crazy?"

"Well, Jeff, do you think you're crazy?"

This always drove me up a wall which is probably good for their business. At any rate, this approach keeps them in control and more importantly they want you to come up with your own solution. If it is you are idea you are more likely to buy into it.

The same applies in sales. Here is how the echo works. You take the last few words of your prospect's comments, and echo it back in the form of a question. So it may sound something like this:

"The problem I have is that I'm not sure how this applies to our situation."

"Your situation?"

"Yea, you know with the merger going on."

"The merger?"

"Yea. It's a real mess. This company from over seas is making an offer on the company and we really don't no where we stand."

"Where you stand?"

"Well, they may want to cut some of the sales force to reduce overhead."

This is a great way to extract information without having to do too much thinking. It gives you the opportunity to figure out the best way to handle the prospect. This is a great way to get information about your members so you can offer products and services you know they need.

When Bill first told me this technique I was excited. I was flying back to Columbus, Ohio from Orlando and thought that a perfect time to try it out was when my girlfriend who later became my wife. She was picking me up at the airport. She always complained that I did not pay to much attention to her which was pretty much on target so I thought this might just help turn things around. I get in the car. Instead of starring off into space as I usually did when I returned from a trip, I turned to her and lead off with a question, "How was work today?"

She was excited. I am paying attention to her and her eyes lit up. "Work was really crazy today. They sent this guy in from the Corporate office to do a quarterly report."

"Quarterly report?"

"Yea. They send someone in every three months or so to make sure we're on target and going to hit our projections."

"Projections?"

"Oh yea. See, last year we were down quite a bit and our quota is to increase the quarter at least 12 percent."

"Twelve percent?"

"At least! If we do it the entire department gets a big bonus!"

"Big bonus?"

"They are going to send on a trip!"

"Trip?"

I kept her going for thirty-five minutes all the way home from the airport. I did not say more than twenty-five words. I knew everything about her life and she very little about mine . . . which was pretty much what I wanted. My echo technique worked. She thought I was the most warm, sensitive, caring individual in the world. One year later

I closed that sale! Then about a year after that we had a little spin off business. About two years ago I got some repeat spinoff business.

As you begin to use it you will get a little more comfortable with it. Be warned, however that if you echo too much some people start to catch on. After about five or six echoes they will look at you with a funny look on their face and say, "what are you . . . and echo?"

So, you might want to alternate it a little using a few other approaches. One that works very much the same way is simply called, "oh?" No matter what the prospect tells you respond with 'oh?', and they come back with more details. You will keep them going for hours if you want to. So the next time you find that your not getting your point across, ask more questions and listen to what the other person is saying.

"Saying?"

Chapter 49

Four Rules for Sales Success

There are four rules to help you analyze your market and attract those customers most likely to buy your products or services, according to Lisa Pinson and Jerry Junnett, authors of the newest edition of *Anatomy of a Business Plan*. They suggest that by focusing your marketing and selling efforts you'll find and keep new customers easier.

Rule #1: Find Customers Who Want Your Product or Service.

If the targeted group of customers already recognizes their need, want, problem, or opportunity, then they're more likely to want to buy your product or service. It's important to note that it's not enough that *you* recognize that your prospects have a need or problem: you'll have to determine if *the group of customers* recognizes this, as well. It's more efficient and cost effective to select a group of potential customers who *already* recognize their need or problem.

To determine which group of customers you should target with your marketing, find out the characteristics of your potential customers that are related to their need or desire for your product or service.

Rule #2: Identify Customers Who Are Ready to Buy.

If your prospects are ready to act to fill their need or solve their problem, then they'll be more likely to buy. Conversely, if your potential customers' need or problem is not strong enough to motivate them to take action, then you'll be forced to market and sell more aggressively to convince them that they'll benefit from filling the need for solving the problem.

We've experienced this when clients hire us to consult with them on how to allocate a limited advertising budget. We're often asked if they should spend more during their peak or off seasons. We generally recommend that they invest their limited ad funds, just prior to, during and perhaps slightly trailing their peak seasons. The reason is that their return on their advertising dollar is higher. In the off-season, you may find that it costs you as many times more to generate a sale.

Rule #3: Tell Customers You Can Fill Their Need.

If your prospects do not yet recognize your ability to meet their need or solve their problem, then you must figure out how to demonstrate your ability to do so. This forms the core of your initial selling activities. If you have chosen a target market segment satisfying Rules #1 and #2, then the bulk of your marketing and sales activities and expenditures will be dedicated to Rules #3 and #4.

Rule #4: Find Customers Who Will Pay.

There are two parts to this Rule:
1. Will your prospects *pay*?
2. Will your prospects *pay you*?

Even though your prospects recognize their need or problem, are motivated to take action, and recognize that you have a solution, they may not be ready, willing or able to pay. You must insure your prospects have the funds budgeted or available to fill this need. You also must insure that you're dealing with the decision-makers.

Smart Selling Action Plan:

• For Success in Sales:

- Find Potential Customers Who Already Want Your Product or Service.
- Identify Customers Who Are Ready to Buy.
- Let the Customers Know that You Can Fill Their Need.
- Find Customers Who Will *Pay You*
- Deal with Decision-Makers.

Chapter 50

Ten Ways To Visit The Non "Visitable"

There are ways to get into see an important prospect when it seems nearly impossible. Pharma Reps have that challenge every day when they visit their assigned doctor's offices. Here are some ways that they have been able to make those visits just a little bit easier.

It has been said that a picture is worth a thousand words. If that is true, then come up with as many Kodak moments with your physicians and their staff as you can. Next time you have a presentation or meeting with an office bring your camera and take pictures of the physician and his/her staff. If you can get yourself in the picture, all the better. Put together a mini photo album and go back into the office and see how much interest there is in seeing the photos. When the doctor or office staff asks to get copies of some of the pictures, say you will bring them in just as soon as you get duplicates made. (Even though you already have duplicates.) This approach is an outstanding method to see this office several times without dropping off samples, or having an appointment.

Holidays are an exceptional excuse to use to get into a doctor's office. Personally handing the doctor a Christmas card, Halloween treat, or even a Valentine rose gives you an opportunity to make an impact with the office and the doctor. The entire office staff and the doctor will appreciate the effort and thoughtfulness in bringing this gift to them.

Aside from the traditional holidays there are the non-traditional holidays you can use as an excuse to visit an office. Think of the interesting ideas you can come up with for Groundhog Day, Secretaries Day, or even National Boss Day. Every month has several non-traditional holidays when you can make an impact in an office. Come up with a creative "excuse" to get into the doctor's office one more time that could make the visit fun.

If the way through the doctor's heart is through his/her stomach, there are many techniques available for any PSR. You can use a wide variety of excuses with food to get into a doctor's office. There is the traditional lunch and learn where you bring lunch in and discuss in detail your products to those in attendance. There are dinner programs, where your company sponsors the dinner and has a speaker discuss your products and answer questions the doctors may have. Another way is just bringing in snacks for the office. This could range from breakfast rolls in the morning, to dessert treats in the afternoon.

In your territory you have a variety of doctors with different religious backgrounds and nationalities. Understanding the different cultures of your physicians gives you the opportunity to make an impression on a particular doctor. You not only get another chance to see the doctor, but also to establish a stronger relationship with that physician. For example, if one of your doctors is Jewish, a nice touch would be to bring in a card commemorating Rosh Hashanah, which is the Jewish New Year. The doctor will appreciate the thoughtfulness of thinking about him/her during one of the holiest holidays.

If you want an opportunity to look like a hero with a certain office, then volunteer to clean their sample closet. The doctor, the office staff and especially the one in charge of maintaining the sample closet will thank-you countless times. This could take a few hours, so is usually done on a Saturday when the office is not busy. Since physicians are usually not busy on Saturdays, they usually come in to inspect the work you're doing. On occasion you will be able to discuss your products with the doctors as you clean their sample closet.

Pharmaceutical selling is a very competitive business. Physicians are inundated with thousands of products and many PSR's. In order to make a difference with those physicians a creative approach is needed. If you can't talk to a decision maker, then you can't sell your product. These 10 techniques give you the ammunition you need get to the physician to make an impact. But reading the information is not going to do it - you need to try these ideas. As NIKE puts it "Just Do It."

Chapter 51

Close More Sales By Knowing Emotional Boundaries

One way to get better results when you're selling is *not* by espousing tons of product knowledge. On the contrary, you may discover that your prospect's or client's are more receptive with you first ask their permission to share your information with them, according to Linda Talley, author of *Business Finesse: Dealing With Sticky Situations in the Workplace for Managers.*

"It's about having emotional boundaries - which most people don't have or honor. If you are the one that is honoring you're client's emotional as well as physical boundaries, they will be more attracted to doing business with you."

We honor physical boundaries such as closed or locked doors, but how often do we honor the emotional boundary? Rarely, especially if we want the customer to do something for us - such as BUY. As a salesperson, you may be three steps ahead of the client but if you don't come back to be with that customer in the present moment, to honor them, you're going to lose them. They won't feel comfortable with you.

Highly Trained Professionals

Most sales people are highly trained professionals and have lots of information and knowledge to give to the customer. Most people have a tendency to *vomit* this information on the customer without asking if that's OK. And usually, that's not OK.

The customer wasn't ready and so they feel uncomfortable - violated. You did not condition the conversation by asking permission.

Conditioning the Conversation

When you ask permission to have the conversation, you honor the other person's boundaries. They will give you a *yes* or *no* answer. When they respond with a yes, they are ready to have a conversation. Until you condition the conversation, you can say anything you want and they may or may not hear it. When they don't hear it and you say it, you have to repeat yourself. Not very productive and very irritating to you. For example: A customer asks you when you can deliver a specific product. You may want to jump in there and say, "First thing next week." Instead, ask permission by saying, "May I tell you?" Get a *yes* or *no* from your customer because when they say yes, that's a key buying signal and you won't be wasting your time. Whenever you have information to give a customer, ask permission. If they don't give it, go back and ask again but don't give your information till you have permission.

SMART SELLING ACTION PLAN

- Begin by practicing this skill at home or in the office - some place that feels safe to try out new sales skills.

- Share this skill with other members of your organization. See how productivity picks up.

- People want information - you want a relationship if you are going to get the sale. Make certain that you have the relationship by asking for more than enough permission.

- Whenever a customer asks a question, ask permission to tell them before you give the information.

- Always get a *yes* or *no* from your customer. If it's *no* you've saved yourself a lot of time.

- Ask for more than enough permission. If you ask and they don't say *yes* or *no*, keep asking till you get an answer. Retrain your customer to want to hear what you have to say.

Chapter 52

Looking The Part
Helps Get the Sale

Early in my sales career, I had a credibility issue with my prospects because I looked so young. So, my goal was to look 15 years older. I realize that may sound a little strange. In an age where both men and women go out of their way to look years younger by packing their faces in mud and vegetables, I have considered spiking my stridex pad just a hint of unleaded and Lava in order to gain a few glorious lines of credibility about my eyes and mouth. Fortunately, I got that brainstorm when gas was over $2.50 a gallon so I looked for another approach.

What's the wrinkle in my story that forever keeps me wishing the same on my face? My age has cost me a lot of money. I started my own company when I was 23 years old. To compound the situation, I'm 5'5" tall and for some reason, many business people equate credibility with age and even height.

Now, some 11 years later, I still look like I'm 18. On many occasions, as I fly around the country to present my Street Fighter seminars some middle aged business looking person next to me on the plane strikes up a conversation that usually ends up with a question like, "So, what's your major?"

I have to admit, now that when I was in my mid 30's and have built up some credentials, its fun. It wasn't, however, in my earlier career when I was struggling to keep my business alive. I found out almost immediately many people in business don't like to engage the services of consultants who look like they could be Peewee Herman's little cousin. My age and youthful appearance has definitely cost me a lot of money.

You would think with all this grief my age has caused that it would make me old before my time. No such luck.

The first real painful experience with my age started after I was hired to help a large restaurant that had some very big problems. it was perhaps four months into the job and things were really moving along. My special local store grassroots marketing and advertising program was just starting to make headway.

To show his appreciation, my client, who very seldom took an active role in this business, asked me to join him for breakfast. I did. The waitress came over carrying two coffee pots and asked us if we wanted coffee. I asked for a Diet Coke. That's what I always drink for breakfast.

"Diet Coke for breakfast. Are you kidding? Don't you drink coffee like normal people?" he asked with a pained look on his face.

I went on to explain that I never acquired a taste for coffee. I was raised in the coffee business ... my parents had a coffee service and vending company and I would make deliveries after school, pack coffee on weekends and basically felt that coffee was ruining my social life. I hated coffee ... wouldn't even eat coffee ice cream. I guess it was a form of teenage rebellion never to drink the stuff. Thank goodness they weren't sex therapists!

For some reason this disturbed him. He took a big sip of his fresh brewed decaf then asked the question that turned out to be my kiss of death, "By the way Jeff, how old are you?"

At the time I really didn't think anything of it. Actually, I was quite proud to have come as far as I did considering how young I was and responded without hesitation, "I'm 23."

The man almost had a coronary on the spot. Here he had entrusted his multi-million dollar operation to a mere child and within the week, I lost my biggest account.

Needless to say, I was devastated ... both emotionally and financially.

But to lose a client, not because I didn't do my job right but because I was too young. This was after he was getting results from my efforts.

Fortunately I recovered quickly. That's one thing I was good at. I realized that it was vital that I use some of my own marketing moxie to solve my credibility problem created by my age. So, I took myself on as a client. This was important because when I work with a client, I always do it fanatically. I remember when I consulted Weight Watchers I took an inch off my waist. After consulting with a Nautilus Fitness Center I added an inch and a half to my biceps. And months after handling a disco, I learned to dance like John Travolta. I did, however, turn down a job from a health clinic in LA specializing in breast enlargements.

To get in the right frame of mind, I signed a contract with myself. I wrote myself a check ... I didn't cash it of course because I knew better. And thus started a campaign to make Jeff look older.

The first thing I did was burn my green polyester leisure suit. Very flammable. Then I had to deal with my car. At the time, I was driving a 1969 Opel GT. This is a little two seater German sports car in two shades of primer grey, faded orange, a ring of rust spots, and one headlamp that was stuck in the "up" position as if the car was winking. Not the kind of car you pick up a 50-year-old millionaire in.

I started looking around for a car that said, "You have to be 40 years old to drive me." At the same time, I didn't want something too fancy and I had to keep my budget in mind ... which was vastly depleted after purchasing my new business suits. I found a brand new Oldsmobile 98 Regency. Instant credibility. This car was huge. I think it slept twelve.

I even had grey put into my hair just around the temples. I know it was extreme, but I was desperate. As a matter of fact, I happened to be at a party where a good friend of the family, a well-known plastic surgeon, was there. I went up to him and asked, "Doc, how much would it cost for a face drop?"

He informed me that the problem would solve itself in time and promptly recommended a good psychologist.

Now I was ready to work on my next 50-year-old millionaire. A potential new client, and I left nothing to chance. I was to pick him up at his office so we could have lunch at his fancy country club to talk business. I pulled into the visitors spot right near the front door of the two story office complex. Before I turned the car off to go inside and get him, I tuned the radio to a beautiful music station ... the kind of lush instrumental elevator music that says, "You have to be 40 years old to listen to me."

After a brief 45-minute wait, we return to my huge car. We get in. On the seat between us is a small bottle of Geritol strategically resting atop the current issue of Modern Maturity magazine next to a box of suppositories. I put the key in the ignition. As the car comes to life, the power antenna rises and the car fills with lush instrumental of Percy Faith playing Stairway to Heaven. After just a few seconds I reach across to turn the radio off so we can begin our business talk, but in just those few seconds, I know I made a very important impression on this gentleman.

Obviously impressed so far, he thoughtfully asked, "By the way Jeff, how old are you?"

It became apparent at that time I had to deal directly with that question of "how old are you". And I had to do it without lying. You never lie to a client. It was a question I struggled with for many weeks than finally the answer hit me. When a client would ask me, "by the way Jeff, how old are you?" I would look them right straight in the eye and respond, "I'll be 37 in April!" This is true. It happens to be in 1993. My mother like it so much she uses it in reverse, "I was 49 in February" (we won't say which February.)

Sneak Preview of
More Smart Marketing

Order Your Copy Onlnie Today:
www.createspace.com/4403184

Chapter 2

Take Care Of Your Customers Now Or Someone Else Will

I go online to place an order for a case of double DVD cases. I've purchased this item many times form this one line vendor as well as CD jewel cases and quad-CD jewel cases. These items are used for the packaging of our various audio and video programs which were converted to the CD format last year. The problem is, this time I don't see the double DVD cases available. I then call the company direct to find out that they no longer carry the type of cases I use. They only carry the deluxe, more expensive version which cost quite a bit more than what we were paying. I was told by the company that the manufacturer discontinued this model. Of course this is upsetting because I have orders to fill and all my packaging inserts were designed around this particular case.

Out of desperation I do a search on Ebay. Eureka! I find several Ebay vendors who carry the same double DVD cases I need. Now I can continue to create my two CD sets. Since I'm still a little peeved at my original vendor, I also search Ebay for the other two types of CD jewel cases I use. Sure enough, there are several other vendors who carry exactly what I use. Plus, the prices for these items are about

151

half of what I was paying before. I chose vendors that have at least a 99% positive rating from past buyers and I place my bids online. Once I win the auction (or use the "buy it now" function to bypass the auction process) I then pay electronically with PayPal. Three days later my orders arrive.

There are a couple of valuable lessons here:

1. From a business buyers' perspective, you should always be looking at other vendors, even if you're happy with your current one. That doesn't mean you should switch right away if you find someone who will sell to you for a few pennies less. But, if your current vendor should, for any reason, not be able to deliver what you need, it's good to have a back up.

2. Also, by shopping around it lets you know that you are still paying a reasonable price for your products or services. If your current vendors are getting complacent in your relationship, they may be charging you too much. It's okay to pay a little more if you know that vendor will service your account as needed. But to pay significantly more when all things appear to be the same is not smart business.

3. You an also use the information you find by shopping around as leverage with your current vendor. Price, service level and other elements can be negotiated if you know what others are offering. For example, if other vendors are offering free shipping and the purchase prices are the same, you would want to bring that to your current vendor's attention.

4. From a sellers' perspective consider this: If you drop a certain product or service it may have negative repercussions that you may not have anticipated. In my experience, the discontinued item caused me to look for another vendor. In that process I found several vendors who offered better prices on all the different items I originally bought from the first vendor. Now that vendor has lost all of my business.

SMART MARKETING ACTION PLAN:

- Think carefully before dropping a product or service from your offerings.

- Comparison shop your current vendors to insure your prices are fair.

- Comparison shop to have a back up vendor just in case.

- Always look at what you offer from your customer's perspective.

- Explore new technologies to replace some you currently offer. We also offer our audio and video programs in both CD/DVD formats and MP3/MP4 downloads. The downloadable version not only is more profitable but a service the clients often prefer.

Chapter 6

Silent Auction Domination

A silent auction is a very popular and productive fund raising event for many organizations. Not only is it a good idea to support worthy causes by donating your products or services, but if you do it right, you can get great exposure. Of course, the big advantage of participating in a silent auction is that you're not donating hard dollars, but your product cost dollars.

Keep in mind that many of your potential customers attend these events, so you want to look for ways to get the most out of your efforts.

Up The Ante

Most businesses generally donate one or two items. However, some of the most popular offerings are those that provide a much higher total value. A few examples of this is the salon that donated one facial a week for a year. That created an item with a retail value of well over $3300, which created a great deal of interest. A local pizza restaurant did a similar thing by offering a large pizza a week for a year. Depending on the type of business you're in, you can really build value by packaging a number of your items into a weekly or monthly item for a year. This would also work easily with things including video rentals, car washes, food items, and so on.

Present Your Best

Many businesses offer items that are left in inventory or no longer popular. While on the surface it may make sense to unload this inventory for worthy cause. From a marketing point of view, you're not getting your bang for the buck. Consider, instead, offering your most popular items. Remember, many people will be exposed to your business name and what you do at these events. You want to make sure the participants associate you and your business with the products and services you want them to buy.

Not So Silent

Once you commit to offer a collection of product and services that have a significant retail value, leverage your donation by negotiating with the emcee to give you so many live mentions during the event. This was done by a jewelry store who donated a $1000 necklace. As part of the arrangement, the event agreed to mention the company and offering 10 times from the microphone and direct people over to his display.

Print The Program

In some smaller events, they may not have a program. If they do, it may not contain advertising. Offer to print their program for them, listing all the items, in exchange for your ad on the back cover. This would be a doubly perfect approach for a printer.

Ticket To Event

If the organization sells tickets to their silent auction, you can offer to print their tickets for them. Furthermore, to help them sell tickets, you offer to put an offer on the back of the ticket that creates additional value. If tickets cost $25, you could offer $25 off the purchase of $100 or more at your business. It gives the impression that each person who buys a ticket gets their money back. Plus, you now have created an impression with everyone who attends the event

Donate The Coffee

Most of these events will offer some kind of beverages or appetizers. If you donate those, you can have a sign up registration or near the food with your company name and logo. It could also get you some mentions live and in the program.

SMART MARKETING ACTION PLAN:

- Donate a popular item.
- Package your services into a big retail value.
- Negotiate for live mentions.
- Provide the program in exchange for advertising.

Learn More Smart Marketing Ideas with this Street Fighter Audio & Video Package

Complete Street Fighter Program

5 Videos (MP4), 15 audios (MP3) and 3 Workbooks (PDF) on <u>one flash drive</u>.

Only $399.00.

Call 800-758-8759.

Index

Made in the USA
San Bernardino, CA
10 February 2016